CAMBRIDGE PRIMARY
Mathematics

Challenge

3

Name:

Contents

Cherri Moseley and Janet Rees

CAMBRIDGE
UNIVERSITY PRESS

University Printing House, Cambridge CB2 8BS, United Kingdom

One Liberty Plaza, 20th Floor, New York, NY 10006, USA

477 Williamstown Road, Port Melbourne, VIC 3207, Australia

4843/24, 2nd Floor, Ansari Road, Daryaganj, Delhi – 110002, India

79 Anson Road, #06–04/06, Singapore 079906

Cambridge University Press is part of the University of Cambridge.

It furthers the University's mission by disseminating knowledge in the pursuit of education, learning and research at the highest international levels of excellence.

www.cambridge.org
Information on this title: www.cambridge.org/9781316509227

First published 2016

20 19 18 17 16 15 14 13 12 11 10 9 8 7 6 5

Printed in Spain by GraphyCems

A catalogue record for this publication is available from the British Library

ISBN 978-1-316-50922-7 Paperback

....

....

This book is part of the Cambridge Primary Maths project. This is an innovative combination of curriculum and resources designed to support teachers and learners to succeed in primary mathematics through best-practice international maths teaching and a problem-solving approach.

To get involved, visit
www.cie.org.uk/cambridgeprimarymaths.

Introduction

This *Challenge activity book* is part of a series of 12 write-in activity books for primary mathematics grades 1–6. It can be used as a standalone book, but the content also complements *Cambridge Primary Maths*. Learners progress at different rates, so this series provides a Challenge and Skills Builder activity book for each Primary Mathematics Curriculum Framework Stage to broaden the depth of and to support further learning.

The *Challenge* books extend learning by providing stretching activities to increase the depth of maths knowledge and skills. Support is given through short reminders of key information, topic vocabulary, and hints to prompt learning. These books have been written to support learners whose first language is not English.

How to use the books

The activities are for use by learners in school or at home, with adult mediation. Topics have been carefully chosen to focus on those areas where learners can stretch their depth of knowledge. The approach is linked directly to *Cambridge Primary Maths*, but teachers and parents can pick and choose which activities to cover, or go through the books in sequence.

The varied set of activities grow in challenge through each unit, including:

- closed questions with answers, so progress can be checked
- questions with more than one possible answer
- activities requiring resources, for example, dice, spinners or digit cards
- activities and games best done with someone else, in class or at home, which give the opportunity for parents and teachers to be fully involved in the child's learning
- activities to support different learning styles: working individually, in pairs or in groups.

How to approach the activities

Space is provided for learners to write their answers in the book. Some activities might need further practice or writing, so students could be given a blank notebook at the start of the year to use alongside the book. Each activity follows a standard structure.

- **Remember** gives an overview of key learning points. It introduces core concepts and, later, can be used as a revision guide. These sections should be read with an adult who can check understanding before attempting the activities.
- **Vocabulary** assists with difficult mathematical terms, particularly when English is not the learner's first language. Learners should read through the key vocabulary with an adult and be encouraged to clarify understanding.

- **Hints** prompt and assist in building understanding, and steer the learner in the right direction.
- **You will need** gives learners, teachers and parents a list of resources for each activity.
- **Photocopiable resources** are provided at the end of the book, for easy assembly in class or at home.
- **Links** to the Cambridge International Examinations Primary Mathematics Curriculum Framework objectives and the corresponding *Cambridge Primary Mathematics Teacher's Resource* are given in the footnote on every page.
- **Calculators** should be used to help learners understand numbers and the number system, including place value and properties of numbers. However, the calculator is not promoted as a calculation tool before Stage 5.

Note:

When a 'spinner' is included, put a paperclip flat on the page so the end is over the centre of the spinner. Place the pencil point in the centre of the spinner, through the paperclip. Hold the pencil firmly and spin the paperclip to generate a result.

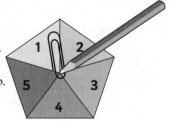

Tracking progress

Answers to closed questions are given at the back of the book – these allow teachers, parents and learners to check their work.

When completing each activity, teachers and parents are advised to encourage self-assessment by asking the students how straightforward they found the activity. When learners are reflecting on games, they should consider how challenging the mathematics was, not who won. Learners could use a ✓/ ✗ or a red/green colouring system to record their self-assessment anywhere on each activity page.

These assessments provide teachers and parents with an understanding of how best to support individual learners' next steps.

Three-digit numbers

Remember

In a three-digit number, the first digit tells you how many hundreds there are in the number, the second digit how many tens and the third digit how many ones. So, for 327, the 3 represents 300, the 2 represents 20 and the 7 represents 7 ones.

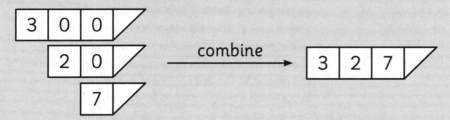

When you add or subtract 10 from a two-digit or three-digit number, the ones digit does not change, for example 134 − 10 = 124, 134 + 10 = 144.

You will need:
resource 1, pages 68–70 – two sets

Vocabulary
hundreds, tens, ones, place value, value

Two children each used a set of place-value cards to make 9 three-digit numbers for an activity.

What is the problem with the two sets of numbers?

Set 1

468	183	769
271	634	859
536	942	315

Set 2

249	765	528
421	157	973
614	382	897

Hint: Use the place-value cards to make both sets of numbers. Can you see what the problem is?

Unit 1A Number and problem solving
CPM Framework 3Nn2, 3Nn3, 3Nn5, 3Nn6, 3Nc9, 3Pt1, 3Pt3, 3Ps3, 3Ps6; CPM Teacher's Resource 1.1

Use a set of place-value cards to make 9 three-digit numbers and record them in the grid.

Write the numbers that are 10 less than each of your numbers in the second grid.

Make these numbers with place-value cards.

Which card is left over? _____

What happens when you write and make the numbers that are 10 more?

Unit 1A Number and problem solving
CPM Framework 3Nn2, 3Nn3, 3Nn5, 3Nn6, 3Nc9, 3Pt1, 3Pt3, 3Ps3, 3Ps6; CPM Teacher's Resource 1.1

5

Remember

The position of a digit in a number tells you its value.

| 3 | 0 | 0 |
| 2 | 0 |
| 7 |

combine → | 3 | 2 | 7 |

You will need:
resource 1,
pages 68–70

Vocabulary
abacus, hundreds, tens, ones, place value, value

You have 12 beads for the abacus.

Make 10 different numbers. Use all of the beads each time.

Then write 10 different numbers that you cannot make with 12 abacus beads.

Hint: Draw the abacus to check how many beads each number needs.

H	T	O

H	T	O

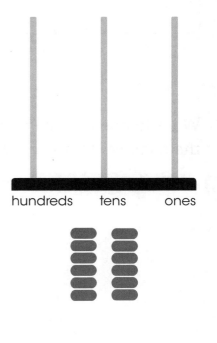

hundreds   tens   ones

Which numbers with 4 tens can you make when you use all 12 beads?

Unit 1A Number and problem solving
CPM Framework 3Nn2, 3Nn3, 3Nn5, 3Nn6, 3Nc10, 3Pt3, 3Ps3, 3Ps6; CPM Teacher's Resource 1.3

Palindromic numbers

Remember

When you add or subtract 10 from a two-digit or three-digit number, the ones digit does not change, for example 134 − 10 = 124, 134 + 10 = 144.

A **palindromic** number is the same when it is written backwards, for example 535.

How many different palindromic numbers are there between 100 and 300? Use the grid to help you record the numbers.

For each palindromic number, write the number that is 10 less and the number that is 10 more.

Which 4 non-palindromic numbers have you made? You will need to continue your grid on another sheet of paper.

10 less	Palindromic number	10 more

Hint: Start with the lowest number you can make and use patterns to find all the possible numbers.

Unit 1A Number and problem solving
CPM Framework 3Nn2, 3Nn3, 3Nn5, 3Nn6, 3Nc9, 3Pt3, 3Ps3, 3Ps6; CPM Teacher's Resource 2.1

7

Phone numbers

Remember

When you add several single-digit numbers, look for number pairs for 10, near pairs, doubles and near doubles to help you.

Make tens then add the tens and ones to find the total.

For example
$$6 + 9 + 4 + 2 + 5 =$$
$$(6 + 4) + (9 + 2) + 5 =$$
$$10 + 11 + 5 = 26$$

Or
$$(5 + 4) + 9 + 2 + 6 =$$
$$9 + 9 + 2 + 6 =$$
$$18 + 2 + 6 = 26$$

1 @?_	2 ABC	3 DEF
4 GHI	5 JKL	6 MNO
7 PQRS	8 TUV	9 WXYZ
*	0	#

Use the letters on a keypad to give each letter a value. Work out the value of each word.

Record in the table. The first word is done for you.

3-letter words		4-letter words	
sum	7 + 8 + 6 = 21	even	
map		hour	
nil		zero	
odd		dice	
day		cube	
add		side	

Hint: Look for number pairs for 10, near pairs, doubles and near doubles to help you add.

Unit 1A Number and problem solving
CPM Framework 3Nn3, 3Nc12, 3Nc16, 3Pt1, 3Pt3, 3Ps3; CPM Teacher's Resource 3.1

5-letter words		6-letter words	
equal		abacus	
array		answer	
count		change	
digit		corner	
money		double	
metre		puzzle	

7-letter words		More than 7 letters	
balance		addition	
between		subtraction	
biggest		multiplication	
compare		division	
largest		rectangle	
explain		quadrilateral	

Include some words of your own.

Is **odd** worth less than **even**?

Is **nil** worth more than **zero**?

Is **dice** worth less than **cube**?

Is **biggest** worth more than **largest**?

What is your name worth? Compare with some friends' names.

Spiders in the bath

Remember
Doubling and halving are the inverse of each other.

Vocabulary
double, half, halve, inverse, operation

When Rebecca and her family left home to go on holiday, there were 3 spiders in their bath.

Each day the number of spiders in the bath doubled. How many spiders were in the bath when Rebecca and her family came home 8 days later? _____

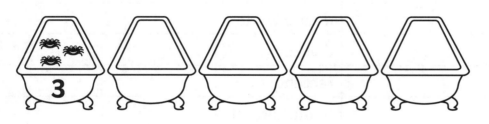

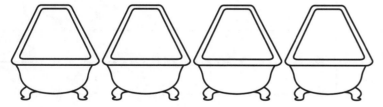

How did you find out?

Unit 1A Number and problem solving
CPM Framework 3Nn3, 3Nn5, 3Nc6, 3Nc7, 3Nc8, 3Nc19, 3Pt1, 3Pt3, 3Ps3, 3Ps6; CPM Teacher's Resource 4.1

Rebecca's dad called in the spider catcher.

He took away half the spiders every day.

How many days was it until there were just 3 spiders left in the bath? _____

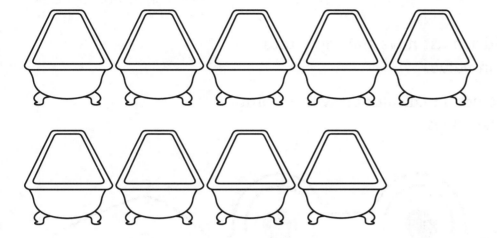

How did you find out?

Hint: To find the double of a two-digit or three-digit number, partition the number into hundreds, tens and ones.
Double each part and then add the parts together to find the double.
To halve a number, partition then halve each part.
Then add the parts together to find half.

Unit 1A Number and problem solving
CPM Framework 3Nn3, 3Nn5, 3Nc6, 3Nc7, 3Nc8, 3Nc19, 3Pt1, 3Pt3, 3Ps3, 3Ps6; CPM Teacher's Resource 4.1

11

Calculating spiders

Remember
Equivalent means of equal value. So 2 + 15 is equivalent in value to 29 − 12; 2 + 15 = 29 − 12.

Vocabulary
value, solve, more, less, worth, addition, total, equivalent, number pair

Each calculation on a spider must have the same total, so each leg is equivalent in value.

Write an addition or subtraction calculation with a total of 17 on each of the spider's legs.

For each spider on page 13:

- choose a number and write it on the body
- write a calculation with that total on each of the legs.

Hint: Use number pairs for the chosen number to get started.

Unit 1A Number and problem solving
CPM Framework 3Nc1, 3Nc11, 3Nc12, 3Pt1, 3Pt3, 3Ps3; CPM Teacher's Resource 5.1, 5.2

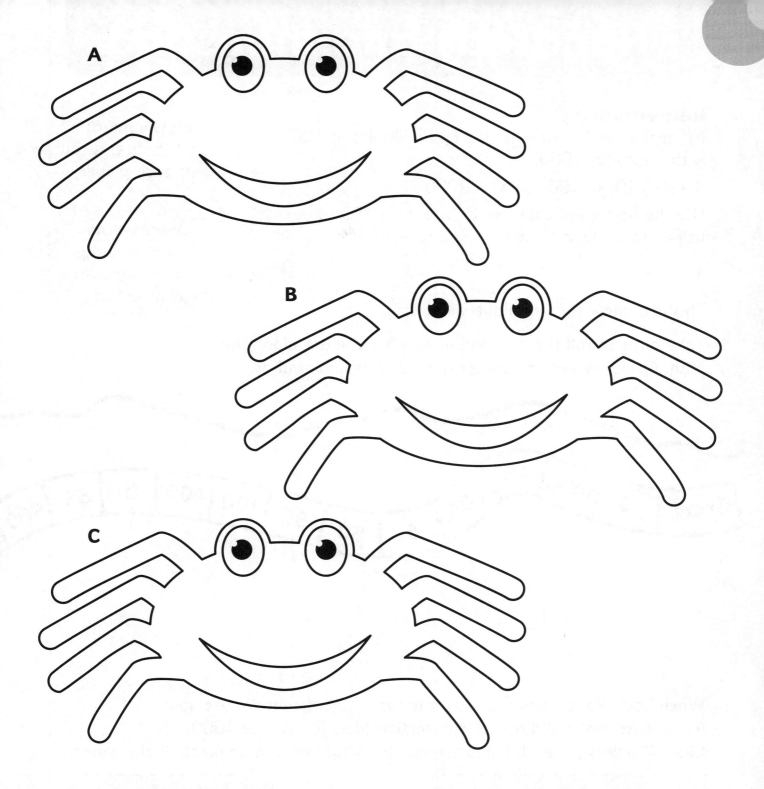

Choose a spider. Write one long calculation showing that each leg is equivalent in value to all the others on that spider.

For example: 2 + 15 = 29 − 12 = ...

Unit 1A Number and problem solving
CPM Framework 3Nc1, 3Nc11, 3Nc12, 3Pt1, 3Pt3, 3Ps3; CPM Teacher's Resource 5.1, 5.2

13

Hundreds and thousands

Remember
Number pairs for 10 help you find multiples of 100 with a total of 1000.

9 + 1 = 10, so 900 + 100 = 1000

Use the pattern of counting in fives on a 100 square to find multiples of 5 that have a total of 100.

You will need:
a 1–6 dice, a counter for each player

Vocabulary
multiple, multiply, total, number pair, number fact

This is a game for two players.

Take turns to roll the dice and move your counter along the path, up the mountain. Collect the numbers you land on.

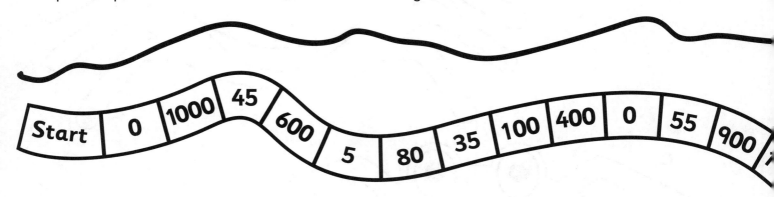

Start | 0 | 1000 | 45 | 600 | 5 | 80 | 35 | 100 | 400 | 0 | 55 | 900

When both players have reached the top of the mountain, use your numbers to make addition or subtraction facts for 100 or 1000.
Claim 2 points for each number fact. The player with more points is the winner.

Player 1's numbers

Player 2's numbers

Unit 1A Number and problem solving
CPM Framework 3Nn2, 3Nn3, 3Nn5, 3Nc1, 3Nc2, 3Nc11, 3Pt1, 3Ps3; CPM Teacher's Resource 5.1

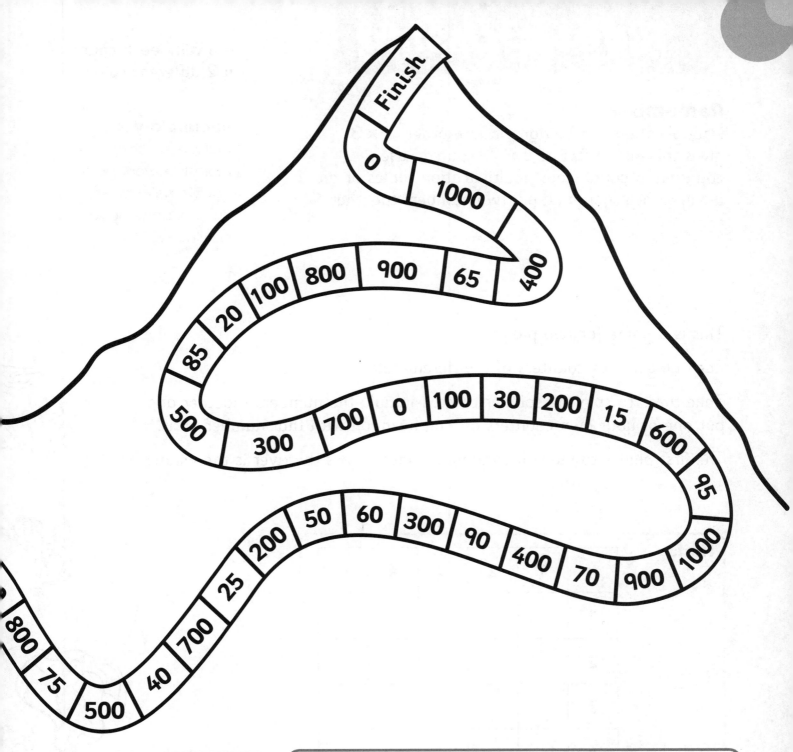

Hint: Use your number pairs for ten to remind you of the multiples of 100 with a total of 1000. Look at the 100 square to remind yourself which two multiples of 5 total 100.

Fact box: Use your numbers to make these number facts. You can use each number only once.

☐ + ☐ = 100   100 − ☐ = ☐

☐ + ☐ = 1000   1000 − ☐ = ☐

Unit 1A Number and problem solving
CPM Framework 3Nn2, 3Nn3, 3Nn5, 3Nc1, 3Nc2, 3Nc11, 3Pt1, 3Ps3; CPM Teacher's Resource 5.1

15

River crossing

Remember

Multiplication can be done in any order. 2 × 3 gives the same total as 3 × 2. You can use counting in equal steps, multiplication tables or an array to help you multiply two numbers together.

Vocabulary

multiple, multiply, solve, more, less, worth, total, double, half, inverse, number pair, equivalent, continuous

This is a game for two players.

Each player uses counters of a different colour.

Take turns to spin the spinner twice. Multiply the numbers together and put one of your own counters on any hexagon with that number on it.

The first player to make a continuous path across the river is the winner.

Hint:

×	1	2	3	4	5
1					
2					
3					
4					
5					

Before playing, complete this 5 by 5 multiplication square to speed up play.
Use patterns and the fact that you can multiply the numbers in any order to help you complete the multiplication square.

Unit 1A Number and problem solving
CPM Framework 3Nn4, 3Nc3, 3Nc4, 3Nc21, 3Nc25, 3Pt1, 3Pt6, 3Ps3, 3Ps5; CPM Teacher's Resource 6.3

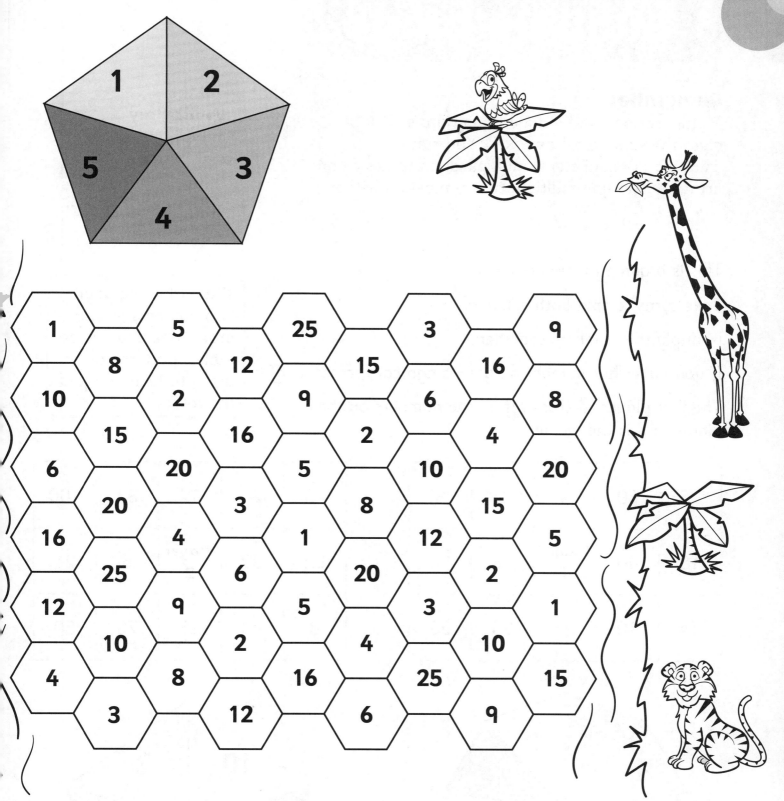

Which numbers are not on the river crossing? Why?

Unit 1A Number and problem solving
CPM Framework 3Nn4, 3Nc3, 3Nc4, 3Nc21, 3Nc25, 3Pt1, 3Pt6, 3Ps3, 3Ps5; CPM Teacher's Resource 6.3

17

Multiple bingo

Remember

Multiplication can be done in any order. 2 × 3 gives the same total as 3 × 2. You can use counting in equal steps, multiplication tables or an array to help you multiply two numbers together.

Vocabulary

multiple, multiply, solve, total

This is a game for two players.

Take turns to spin both spinners.

Multiply the numbers together.

If you have that number on your bingo card, cross it off.

The first player to cross off all the numbers on their bingo card is the winner.

Hint: Multiply your two numbers in any order. Use your times tables, patterns or an array to help you find the total.

25	60	4	26	9
18	40	Player 1	16	80
14	10	27	20	28

45	24	12	35	100
32	30	Player 2	6	21
8	90	15	70	50

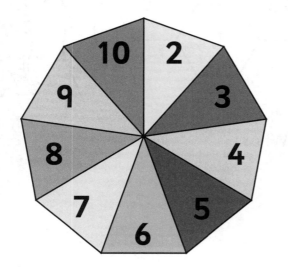

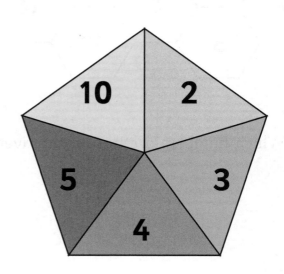

Unit 1A Number and problem solving
CPM Framework 3Nn4, 3Nc3, 3Nc4, 3Nc21, 3Nc25, 3Pt1, 3Pt6, 3Ps3; CPM Teacher's Resource 6.3

Multiples of 3 and 4

Remember
Start counting at zero and count in steps of equal size to find multiples of the step size. 3, 6, 9, 12, 15 ... are all multiples of 3.

Vocabulary
multiple, multiply, Venn diagram

Complete the Venn diagram.

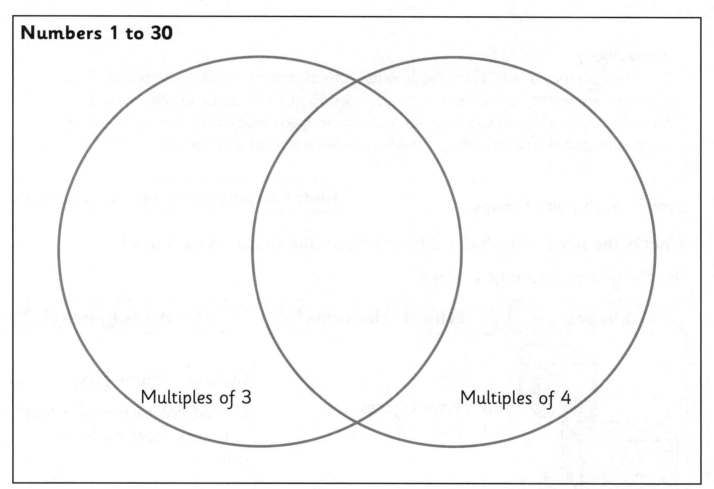

Numbers 1 to 30

Multiples of 3

Multiples of 4

What can you say about the numbers in the overlap?

Draw your own Venn diagram. Find a way to label your diagram so that there are no numbers in the overlap.

Hint: Check whether each number is a multiple of 3, then 4.

Unit 1A Number and problem solving
CPM Framework 3Dh3, 3Nn4, 3Nc3, 3Nc4, 3Ps5, 3Ps6; CPM Teacher's Resource 6.1

Same and different

Remember

Two-dimensional (2D) shapes are flat and have no depth. Properties include sides and vertices.

Three-dimensional (3D) shapes are solids with length, height and depth. Properties include faces, vertices and edges. 3D shapes have 2D shape faces.

You will need: some 2D and 3D shapes

Vocabulary

2D shape, 3D shape, side, face, edge, vertex, vertices, triangle, square, rectangle, quadrilateral, pentagon, hexagon, octagon, decagon, circle, sphere, cube, cuboid, cylinder, cone, square-based pyramid, triangular-based pyramid, triangular-based prism, hexagonal-based prism, octahedron, icosahedron, dodecahedron

Look at each pair of shapes.

Hint: Compare faces, vertices and edges.

What is the same and what is different about the shapes in each pair?

Use the grid to record your ideas.

Shapes	What is the same?	What is different?
	Both have 6 faces and 12 edges.	Cube has square faces. Cuboid has rectangular faces, but some faces could be squares.

Unit 1B Geometry and problem solving
CPM Framework 3Gs3, 3Gs4, 3Gs6, 3Pt9; CPM Teacher's Resource 7.2

Shapes	What is the same?	What is different?
Choose two 3D shapes to compare. Write their names here.		

Squares and triangles

Remember

2D shapes with straight sides may be **regular** or **irregular**. In a regular shape, all the sides are equal and all the angles are equal. 2D shapes with five or more straight sides are named by the number of sides or corners (vertices).

You will need: resource 2, page 71, scissors, glue

Vocabulary
triangle, square, rectangle, quadrilateral, pentagon, hexagon, octagon, decagon

Cut out squares or equilateral triangles with sides 2 cm long. Use them to make rectangles, pentagons, hexagons, octagons and decagons. The shapes must touch along one side. Do not mix squares and triangles. Some of your shapes will be regular, some will be irregular. Glue the shapes to the page and name them.

Hint: Count the sides to help you name the shape.

Unit 1B Geometry and problem solving
CPM Framework 3Dh2, 3Gs1, 3Gs2, 3Gs6, 3Pt8; CPM Teacher's Resource 7.1

Complete the frequency table to show how many of each shape you have made when you have finished.

Name your quadrilaterals.

Shape (regular or irregular)	Tally	Frequency
quadrilateral		
pentagon		
hexagon		
octagon		
decagon		

Shape match

You will need: 3D shapes, a 1–6 dice, counters in two different colours

Remember

Three-dimensional (3D) shapes have length, height and depth. Their properties include faces, vertices and edges.

Vocabulary

cube, cuboid, cylinder, cone, sphere, square-based pyramid, triangular-based pyramid, triangular-based prism, hexagonal-based prism, octahedron, icosahedron, dodecahedron, faces, vertices, edges, identical

This is a game for two players.

Take turns to roll the dice.

Check your score with the key.

Place one of your counters on a shape that matches the key for that number.

If there is no shape to match the number rolled, miss a turn. Continue until all the shapes are covered.

The winner is the player with counters on more shapes at the end of the game.

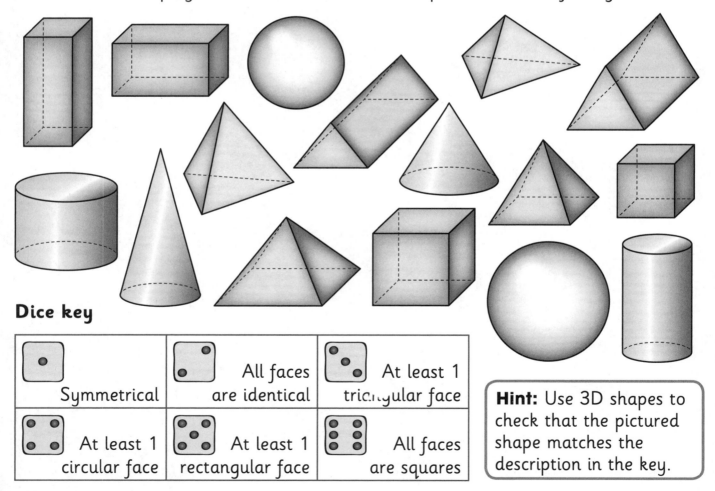

Dice key

Symmetrical	All faces are identical	At least 1 triangular face
At least 1 circular face	At least 1 rectangular face	All faces are squares

Hint: Use 3D shapes to check that the pictured shape matches the description in the key.

Unit 1B Geometry and problem solving
CPM Framework 3Gs3, 3Gs4, 3Gs6, 3Gs7, 3Pt9; CPM Teacher's Resource 7.2

Planet Xylo

You will need:
3D shapes

Remember

Three-dimensional (3D) shapes have faces, vertices and edges.

Vocabulary
cube, cuboid, square-based pyramid, triangular-based pyramid, triangular-based prism, hexagonal-based prism, octahedron, icosahedron, dodecahedron

People on Planet Xylo use 3D shapes as money. A return ticket on the interplanetary transporter to Planet Xylo costs 24 faces.

You need 6 tickets to Planet Xylo and each ticket must be different!

Which shapes could you use to buy each ticket?

Either draw the shapes or write the shape names on each ticket.

One has been done for you.

Hint: Check the number of faces on each shape before you start making the tickets.

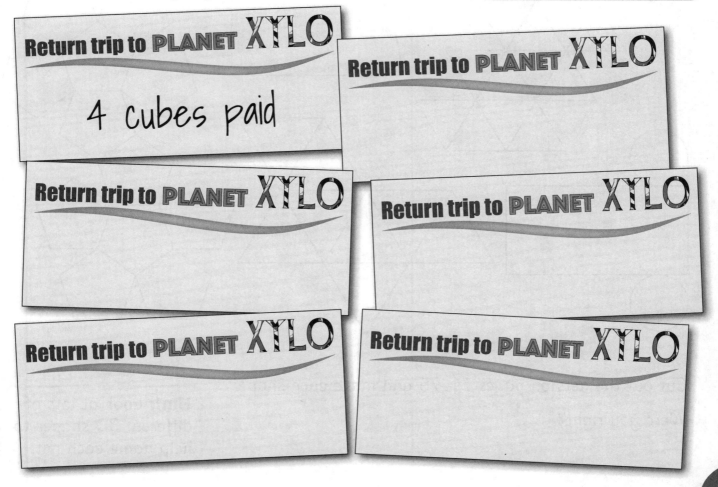

Return trip to PLANET XYLO

4 cubes paid

Return trip to PLANET XYLO

Return trip to PLANET XYLO

Return trip to PLANET XYLO

Return trip to PLANET XYLO

Return trip to PLANET XYLO

Nets

Remember
A **net** is a 2D plan of a 3D shape. You can cut out the net and fold it to make the 3D shape.

You will need:
resource 3, pages 72–75, scissors, glue

Vocabulary
net, triangle, square, rectangle, quarilateral, pentagon, hexagon, octagon, decagon, circle, sphere, cube, cuboid, cylinder, cone, square-based pyramid, triangular-based pyramid, triangular-based prism, hexagonal-based prism, octahedron, icosahedron, dodecahedron

Predict which shape each net will make.

Cut out the nets on pages 71–75 and make each shape.

Were you right?

Hint: Look at lots of different 3D shapes to help name each net.

Unit 1B Geometry and problem solving
CPM Framework 3Gs3, 3Gs4, 3Gs6, 3Pt8, 3Pt9; CPM Teacher's Resource 7.3

Symmetrical flags

Remember
Symmetrical shapes may have more than one line of symmetry.

You will need: a ruler, a mirror

Vocabulary
flag, symmetry, line of symmetry

Each flag has 0, 1 or 2 lines of symmetry.
Draw the lines of symmetry on each flag and write how many lines you found.

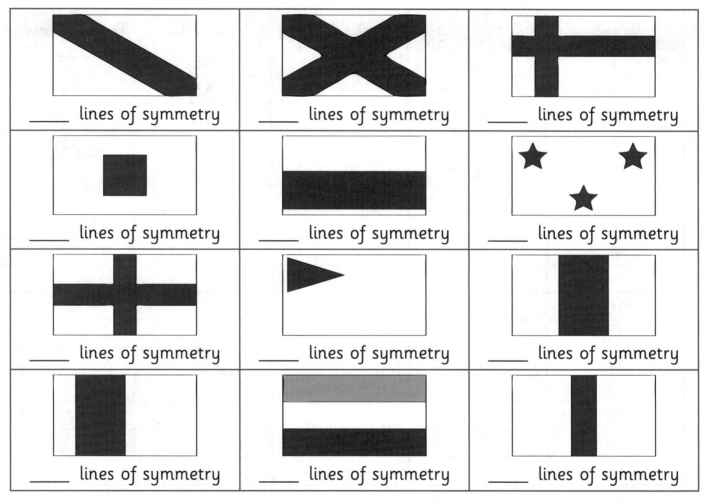

_____ lines of symmetry   _____ lines of symmetry   _____ lines of symmetry

_____ lines of symmetry   _____ lines of symmetry   _____ lines of symmetry

_____ lines of symmetry   _____ lines of symmetry   _____ lines of symmetry

_____ lines of symmetry   _____ lines of symmetry   _____ lines of symmetry

Now draw 3 flags, one with no lines of symmetry, one with 1 line
of symmetry and one with 2 lines of symmetry.

Hint: Use the mirror to check for lines of symmetry.

Pocket money

Would you rather have $5 pocket money every week or start with 1c and have it doubled every week? Which would give you the greater amount after 20 weeks? Use the table to help you.

Week	Doubling	Total received	$5 a week	Total received
1	1c	1c	$5	$5
2	2c	3c	$5	$10
3	4c	7c	$5	$15
4	8c	15c	$5	$20
5	16c		$5	
6				
7				
8				
9				
10				
11				
12				
13				
14				
15				
16				
17				
18				
19				
20				

Hint: Convert cents to dollars to make the larger amounts easier to double. Estimate each double before you work it out.

Unit 1C Measure and problem solving
CPM Framework 3Nc14, 3Mm1, 3Ps4, 3Pt10; CPM Teacher's Resource 9.1

How old?

Remember
There are 60 minutes in an hour, 24 hours in a day, 7 days in a week, 52 weeks in a year, 365 days in a year (366 in a leap year). There are 28, 29, 30 or 31 days in a month, depending on the month and whether or not it is a leap year.

You will need: a calendar

Vocabulary
minute, hour, day, week, month, year, leap year

When were you born? Use a calendar to help you work out how old you are in years, months and days.

Are you older or younger than each of these people?

I am 7½ years old.

I am 90 months old.

I am 400 weeks old.

I am 7 years and 180 days old.

I am 3000 days old.

I am 2800 days old.

I am 4 million minutes old.

I am 92 months and 9 days old.

I am 70 000 hours old.

Hint: Work out how many years, how many months, how many days and how many minutes have passed since you were born to help you to compare with the time periods.

Unit 1C Measure and problem solving
CPM Framework 3MI5, 3Mt1, 3Mt4, 3Pt1, 3Pt2, 3Pt3, 3Pt11, 3Pt12, 3Ps2, 3Ps3; CPM Teacher's Resource 10.2

Fill up!

Remember
There are 1000 ml in every litre.

Vocabulary
millilitre, litre

This is a two player game.

Take turns to roll the dice. Check the key and add that much water to your container.

Dice key

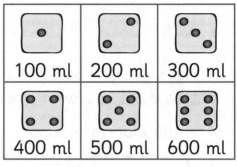

100 ml	200 ml	300 ml
400 ml	500 ml	600 ml

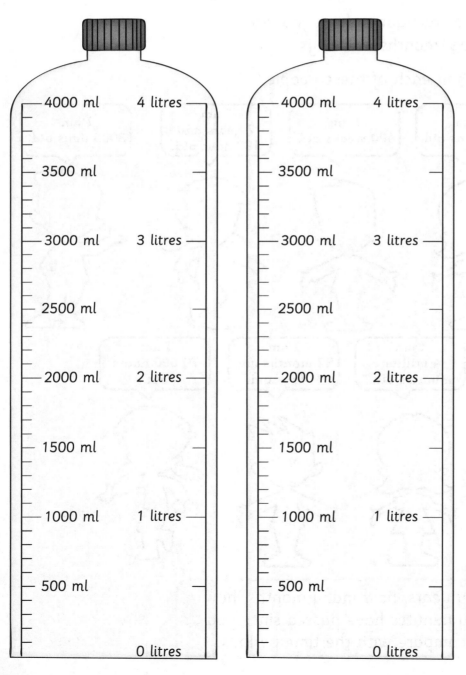

Use a blue pencil to draw the level of the water.

The winner is the first player to fill their container with exactly 4 litres of water.

No spills allowed – if you roll an amount that is more than you need, you must miss that turn.

Record each addition that you make to your container. Check that these add up to the correct total, to confirm the winner.

Hint: Use a ruler to draw the height of the water across the container. Check both scales.

Unit 1C Measure and problem solving
CPM Framework 3MI1, 3MI2, 3MI3, 3Mt1, 3Pt2, 3Pt12; CPM Teacher's Resource 11.1

Cross-number puzzle

Remember
When adding or subtracting 10, the ones digit does not change. When adding or subtracting 100, the tens and ones digits do not change.

You will need:
resource 1,
pages 68–70

Vocabulary
digit, hundreds, tens, ones, more than, less than

Solve each clue and write the number in the correct place to complete the cross number. Write each digit in a different square.

Cross-number clues

Across
1. 10 more than 358
2. 100 less than 831
3. 200 less than 297
4. 110 less than 2 across
5. 10 more than 399
7. 10 more than 4 down
8. 300 less than 342
9. 10 more than 4 across
10. 100 more than 8 down
11. 700 less than 2 across
12. 380 less than 5 across

Down
1. 10 less than 404
2. 100 less than 6 down
4. 10 more than 592
5. 2 more than 5 across
6. 10 less than 839
7. 100 less than 2 across
8. 20 less than 479
9. 120 less than 183
10. 200 less than 252

Hint: Use place-value cards to help you add or subtract.

Unit 2A Number and problem solving
CPM Framework 3Nn2, 3Nn3, 3Nn5, 3Nn6, 3Nc9, 3Nc10, 3Nc18, 3Pt1, 3Ps3; CPM Teacher's Resource 12.1

31

On the way home

Remember

When you multiply by 10, each one becomes a ten and each 10 become a hundred. A zero is needed in the ones space to ensure that each digit is in the correct place for its value.

hundreds	tens	ones
	6	7
6	7	0

You will need: a 1–6 dice, two counters, a bank of real or replica coins and notes

Vocabulary
cent, dollar, times, multiply

Unit 2A Number and problem solving
CPM Framework, 3Nn5, 3Nn7, 3Nc3, 3Nc20, 3Nc21, 3Pt1, 3Ps2; CPM Teacher's Resource 12.3

Take turns to roll the dice and move your counter along the track from school to home.

If you land on a square with an amount in it, collect 10 times that amount from the bank. If you do not have coins and notes, record the amounts and add them up as you collect them.

The winner is the player who arrives home with more money.

Hint: Multiply the number of cents you land on by 10. If the amount is more than 100c, collect it in dollars and cents. Sort the notes and coins into different denominations to help you count them or total the amounts by adding on each time you collect some money.

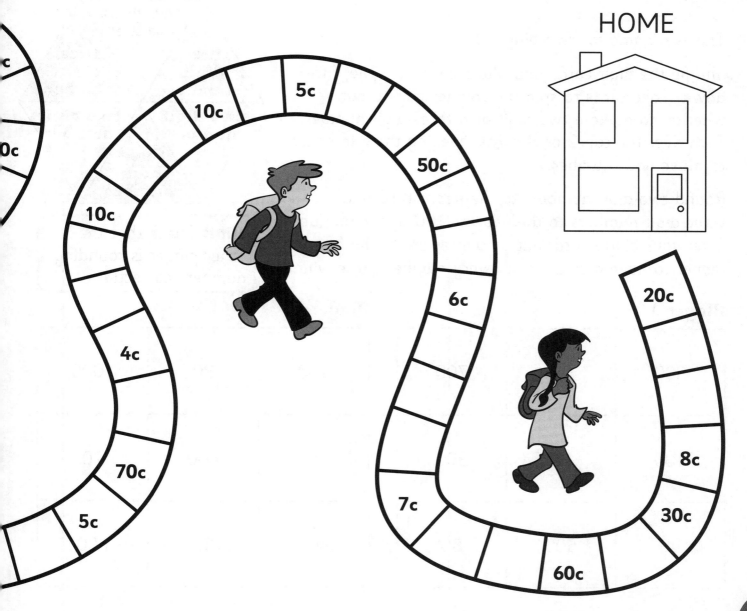

HOME

Unit 2A Number and problem solving
CPM Framework, 3Nn5, 3Nn7, 3Nc3, 3Nc20, 3Nc21, 3Pt1, 3Ps2; CPM Teacher's Resource 12.3

33

Rounding bingo

You will need: resource 4, page 76

Vocabulary
round, rounding

Remember

To round a two-digit number to the nearest 10, look at the ones digit. If it is 1, 2, 3 or 4, round down to the tens number of the original number. If it is 5, 6, 7, 8 or 9, round up to the next tens number. The ones digit will be 0.

To round a three-digit number to the nearest 100, look at the tens digit. If it is 1, 2, 3 or 4, round down to the hundreds number of the original number. If it is 5, 6, 7, 8 or 9, round up to the next hundreds number. The tens and ones digits will be 00.

This is a game for two players.

Shuffle the digit cards and place them in a pile, face down. Take turns to spin the spinner to find out whether to make a two-digit or a three-digit number. Turn over the top 2 or 3 cards, keeping them in order, to make your number.

Round two-digit numbers to the nearest 10 and three-digit numbers to the nearest 100. If the number is on your bingo card, put a counter on it. The first player to have a counter on every number is the winner.

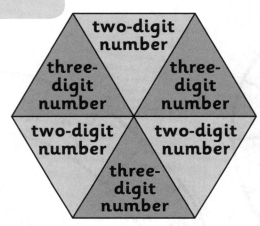

Hint: Check that the other player is rounding numbers correctly.

Player 1

900	20	700
100	60	300
40	500	80

Player 2

200	30	1000
90	400	70
800	50	600

Unit 2A Number and problem solving
CPM Framework 3Nn2, 3Nn5, 3Nn8, 3Pt1, 3Pt12, 3Ps6; CPM Teacher's Resource 13.1

Single, double, treble, quadruple

Remember

Single means once, **double** means twice, **treble** means three times and **quadruple** means four times.

Vocabulary

single, double, treble, quadruple, multiply, multiplication

When you double, treble and quadruple each single-digit number, which even numbers below 30 are never made?

Use the grid to help you find out.

Single (× 1)	1	2	3	4	5	6	7	8	9
Double (× 2)						12			
Treble (× 3)	3			12					
Quadruple (× 4) (or double the double)			12						

Not in grid [   ]

> **Hint:** To quadruple a number, double the double.

Odd one out

You will need: a number line (optional)

Remember

There are many different ways of adding and subtracting. You can do this mentally by looking for number pairs, near number pairs, doubles or near doubles, count on or back, draw jumps on a number line, use place value or something else.

To check an addition is correct, add in a different order or take one of the two numbers away from the total. To check a subtraction, add the answer to the smaller number.

Vocabulary
addition, calculation, equivalent, row subtraction

Hint: You can add or subtract in any way you choose. Check all 4 calculations in each row to be sure you have ringed the correct calculation.

On each row, three calculations are equivalent and one is not. Draw a ring around the odd calculation out in each row.

1	39 + 29	41 + 27	84 – 7	80 – 12
2	132 – 60	28 + 45	89 – 17	36 + 36
3	73 + 74	166 – 9	148 + 9	95 + 62
4	242 + 19	207 + 54	269 + 8	254 + 7
5	79 + 56	92 – 69	81 – 58	65 – 42
6	27 + 58	64 + 21	49 + 46	99 – 14
7	298 + 7	313 – 8	297 + 8	302 + 4
8	99 – 6	41 + 53	100 – 6	103 – 9
9	505 – 9	423 + 83	451 + 45	502 – 6
10	32 + 27	83 – 24	91 – 32	29 + 29

Choose any row. Show how you worked out each calculation.

Unit 2A Number and problem solving
CPM Framework 3Nn2, 3Nn5, 3Nc14, 3Nc15, 3Nc16, 3Nc17, 3Pt1, 3Pt4, 3Pt5, 3Ps3; CPM Teacher's Resource 15.1, 15.2, 15.3

Division tables

Remember
Division is the inverse of multiplication.

Vocabulary
multiplication, division, inverse, remainder

Look at these multiplication and division tables for 3.

$1 \times 3 = 3$	$3 \div 3 = 1$
$2 \times 3 = 6$	$6 \div 3 = 2$
$3 \times 3 = 9$	$9 \div 3 = 3$
$4 \times 3 = 12$	$12 \div 3 = 4$
$5 \times 3 = 15$	$15 \div 3 = 5$
$6 \times 3 = 18$	$18 \div 3 = 6$
$7 \times 3 = 21$	$21 \div 3 = 7$
$8 \times 3 = 24$	$24 \div 3 = 8$
$9 \times 3 = 27$	$27 \div 3 = 9$
$10 \times 3 = 30$	$30 \div 3 = 10$
$11 \times 3 = 33$	$33 \div 3 = 11$
$12 \times 3 = 36$	$36 \div 3 = 12$

Look at the division table.

If you divide any number below 36 that is not a multiple of 3 by 3 you will have a remainder.

$$11 \div 3 = 3 \text{ r}2$$
$$17 \div 3 = 5 \text{ r}2$$
$$28 \div 3 = 9 \text{ r}1$$

Choose a multiplication table you know well.

Write the division table **without** writing the multiplication tables.

Now choose a second multiplication table that you know less well.

Try to write the division table **without** writing the multiplication table.

Use each division table to help you write 3 division calculations with remainders.

Hint: Say the multiplication table to yourself as you write the division table.

Multiplication pyramids

Vocabulary
multiply, multiplication

Remember
You can multiply numbers in any order.
2 × 3 gives the same total as 3 × 2.

In a multiplication pyramid, you multiply the numbers that are next to each other in the row to make the number above them.

Complete the pyramids.

The first one has been done for you.

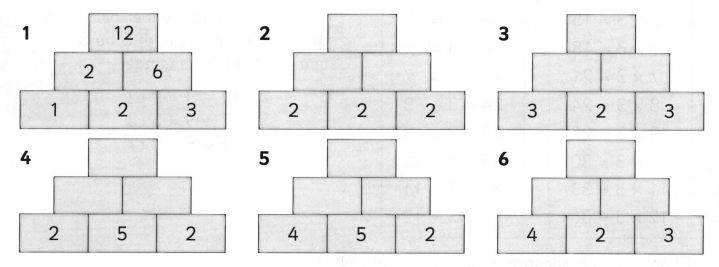

1
12
2 — 6
1 — 2 — 3

2
2 — 2 — 2

3
3 — 2 — 3

4
2 — 5 — 2

5
4 — 5 — 2

6
4 — 2 — 3

Only the top number is shown in each of these multiplication pyramids.
Complete each pyramid.

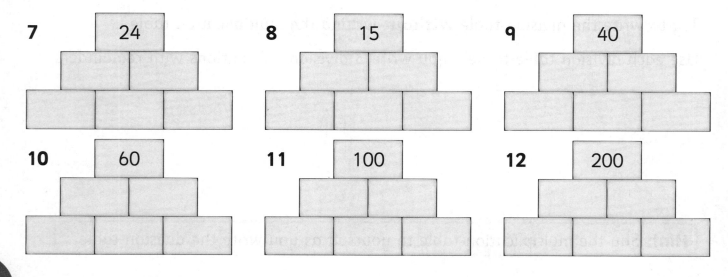

7 24

8 15

9 40

10 60

11 100

12 200

Unit 2A Number and problem solving
CPM Framework 3Nn4, 3Nc3, 3Nc4, 3Nc21, 3Nc22, 3Nc23, 3Nc25, 3Nc26, 3Pt1, 3Ps3; CPM Teacher's Resource 16.1, 16.2, 16.3

These multiplication pyramids have four rows, with four bricks in the bottom row. Choose your own numbers then complete each pyramid.

Unit 2A Number and problem solving
CPM Framework 3Nn4, 3Nc3, 3Nc4, 3Nc21, 3Nc22, 3Nc23, 3Nc25, 3Nc26, 3Pt1, 3Ps3; CPM Teacher's Resource 16.1, 16.2, 16.3

39

The early bird catches the worm

Remember
There are 60 minutes in an hour.
Times between midnight and midday are called am, times between midday and midnight are called pm.

You will need: a 1–6 dice, counters, analogue and digital clocks

Vocabulary
time, minutes, analogue clock, digital clock, earlier, later, am, pm

Take turns to roll the dice and move your counter that many spaces. If you land on a worm, use the spinner to find out what time it is and answer the time question. If your answer is yes, move on or back as instructed. If your answer is no, stay where you are. The first player to reach finish is the winner.

Hint: Set your clock to the time on the spinner to help you answer the time questions. Check for am and pm.

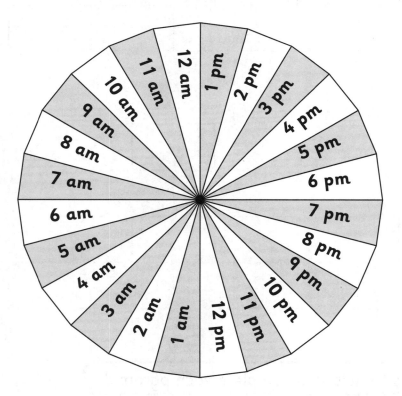

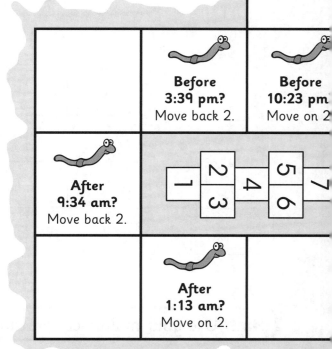

Before 3:39 pm? Move back 2.

Before 10:23 pm? Move on 2

After 9:34 am? Move back 2.

After 1:13 am? Move on 2.

1 2 3 4 5 6 7

Unit 2B Measure and problem solving
CPM Framework 3Mt2, 3Pt2; CPM Teacher's Resource 17.1, 17.2

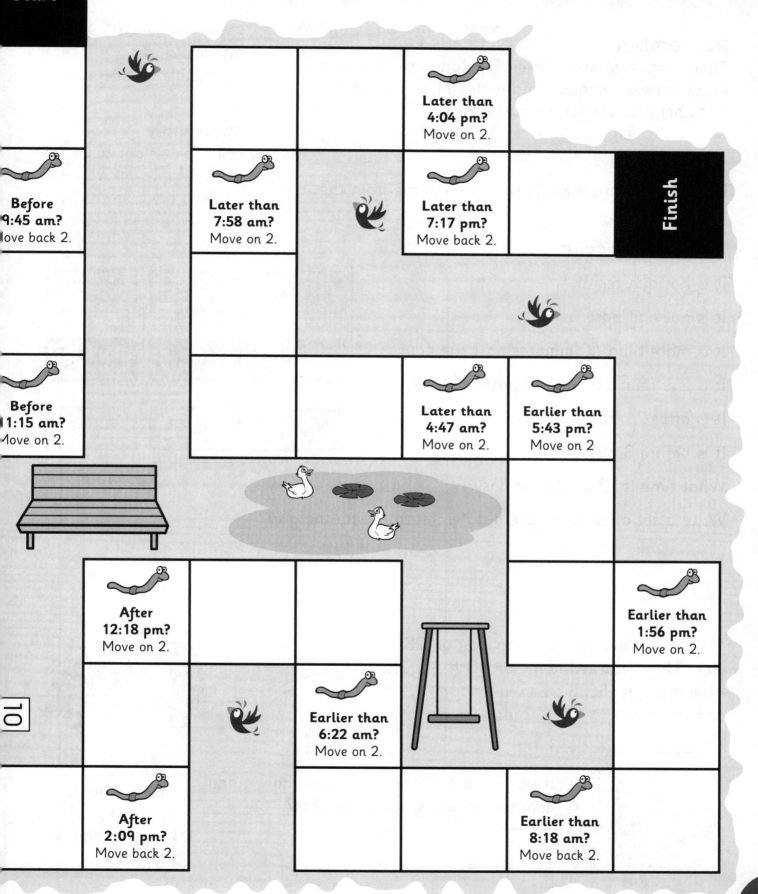

Start

Finish

Before
9:45 am?
Move back 2.

Before
1:15 am?
Move on 2.

Later than
4:04 pm?
Move on 2.

Later than
7:58 am?
Move on 2.

Later than
7:17 pm?
Move back 2.

Later than
4:47 am?
Move on 2.

Earlier than
5:43 pm?
Move on 2

After
12:18 pm?
Move on 2.

Earlier than
1:56 pm?
Move on 2.

Earlier than
6:22 am?
Move on 2.

After
2:09 pm?
Move back 2.

Earlier than
8:18 am?
Move back 2.

10

A question of time

Remember

Times between midnight and midday are called am, times between midday and midnight are called pm. Both periods last for 12 hours.

You will need:
digital clocks if available, a calendar

Vocabulary

time, minutes, analogue clock, digital clock, earlier, later, am, pm, quarter past, half past, quarter to

Uses the clues to identify the correct time from the digital clocks.

It is not quarter past.

It is not quarter to.

It is not half past.

It is more than 40 minutes past the hour.

It is less than 50 minutes past the hour.

It is after 7 o'clock.

It is before 8 o'clock.

What time is it? Circle the answer.

Write a set of clues to give a different time from the grid.

The Chen family went on holiday on 28th July. They returned home on 13th August. How many nights were they away?

If you sleep for 8 hours a night, how many minutes do you sleep in 2 nights?

Hint: Check one piece of information at a time.

Unit 2B Measure and problem solving
CPM Framework 3Mt2, 3Mt3, 3Mt4, 3Pt2; CPM Teacher's Resource 17.1, 17.2

Days and dates

You will need:
a calendar

Remember

There are seven days in a week. The days of the week always follow the same order.

Vocabulary

Monday, Tuesday, Wednesday, Thursday, Friday, Saturday, Sunday

Today is Thursday.

What day of the week will it be:

5 days from today? _____

11 days from today? _____

21 days from today? _____

40 days from today? _____

70 days from today? _____

Sami had 4 weeks holiday.
She went to France for 18 days, then camping in Scotland for 9 days.
How many days holiday did she have left?

_____

There are 30 days in April. Sibo's birthday was on 23rd April.
What is the date 3 weeks after his birthday?

_____

Hint: Count on using the regular order of the days of the week to find a new day or date.

Estimate and measure

Remember

100 cm = 1 metre

1000 metres = 1 kilometre

1000 millilitres = 1 litre

1000 grams = 1 kilogram

1 litre jug marked in 100 ml

You will need: a 30 cm ruler and a metre stick, 1 g and 1 kg weights or kitchen type scales, a litre jug with clear scale

Vocabulary

centimetre, metre, kilometre, gram, kilogram, millilitre, litre, estimate

Draw a ring around the best estimate for each measurement.

Length of a car

1 metre   4 metres   8 metres

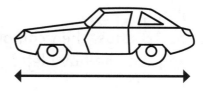

Capacity of a mug

3 litres   30 millilitres   300 millilitres

Height of an elephant

30 centimetres   3 metres   3 kilometres

Unit 2B Measure and problem solving
CPM Framework 3MI1, 3MI2, 3MI5, 3Pt2, 3Pt12; CPM Teacher's Resource 18.1, 18.2

Weight of an egg

6 grams   60 grams   600 grams

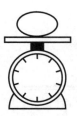

Length of a mobile phone

5 centimetres   12 centimetres   20 centimetres

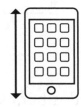

Weight of an apple

100 grams   10 grams   1 kilogram

Capacity of a teapot

1 millilitre   1 litre   10 litres

Weight of a new born baby

40 kilograms   400 grams   4 kilograms

Capacity of a bath

400 millilitres   4 litres   200 litres

Hint: Picture the object alongside the relevant measuring instruments.

Money problems

Remember
100c = $1

 = **$1**

You will need:
banknotes and coins
(optional)

Vocabulary
cent, dollar

Ravi's mother opened a bank account for him.

On the first day of every month she put $30 into the account.

Each month Ravi took out half of what was in the account.

How much money was in the account after three months?

What if Ravi's mother put in $24? Or $36? Or $40?

Natalia needed some stamps for her postcards.

She had $2 and bought some 19c stamps and some 25c stamps.

She had 49c change.

How many of each stamp did she buy?

> **Hint:** Work out one step at a time.

Unit 2B Measure and problem solving
CPM Framework 3Nc14, 3Mm1, 3Mm2, 3Pt2, 3Pt10; CPM Teacher's Resource 19.1, 19.2

Holiday time

There are 2 adults and 3 children in your family.

Your family has $700 to spend on holiday flights. Where can they go?

Vocabulary
money, dollars, spend, cost

Flight costs						
Place	Turkey	Greece	Cyprus	Italy	Spain	Portugal
Adult	$199	$189	$179	$209	$204	$201
Child	$99	$109	$119	$104	$97	$95

Use this space for working out.

Hint: Add amounts of money together in the same way that you would add numbers.

At the funfair

Remember

Tallies are marks to help you count. You make a mark for every item, but you draw every fifth mark across the previous four. Then you count in fives for the completed groups and count the rest in ones.

This ||||| | is a tally for 6 and

this ||||| ||||| || is a tally for 12.

The **frequency** is the number of times something happens. You usually record this in a frequency table. You can use a bar graph to compare frequencies for each category by comparing the lengths of the bars.

Vocabulary

tally, tally chart, frequency table, bar chart

These are the results of a survey of the most popular rides at the funfair from 3 pm to 4 pm.

Complete the tally chart and frequency table.

Ride	Tally	Frequency
Carousel	||||| ||||| ||||| |||	
Bumper cars	||||| ||||| |||||	
Ferris wheel		23
Helter skelter		14
Roller coaster		28
Teacups	||||| ||||| ||	
Waltzers		21
Drop tower	||||| ||||| ||||| ||||| ||||| |||||		
Pirate ship		27

Unit 2C Handling data and problem solving
CPM Framework 3Dh1, 3Dh2, 3Ps4; CPM Teacher's Resource 20.2, 20.3

Complete the matching bar chart.

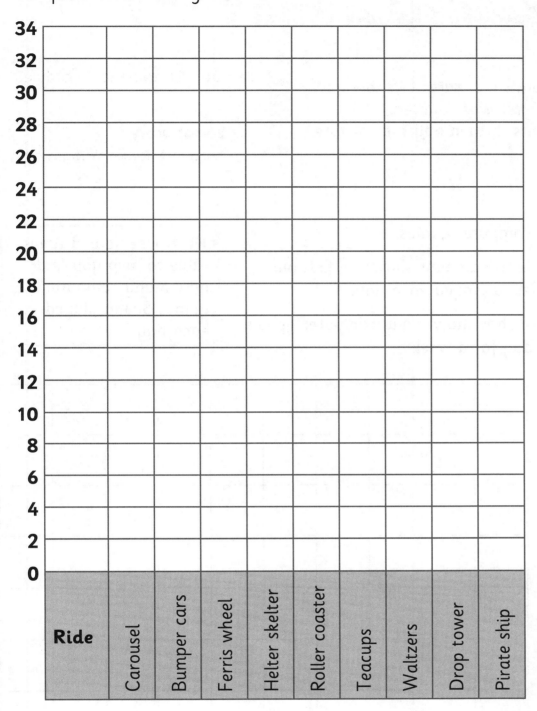

Hint: Check the scale on the bar chart to be sure you colour the correct number of squares.

The fair owners want to close 3 rides in the afternoons.
Which rides would you advise them to close? Why?

Computer games

Remember
In a **pictogram** you use pictures to show how many times each object was counted.
If a picture represents 2, then half that picture represents 1.

You will need: a 1–6 dice

Vocabulary
frequency table, pictogram

Selma likes to play computer games.

Roll a dice and treble the amount shown to find out how many games Selma played each day.

Draw a pictogram to show how many computer games Selma played each day for a week.

Hint: Use your 3 times table to help you find how many computer games Selma played each day.

= 2

=1

Which day or days did she play the most games?

Which day or days did she play the fewest games?

Unit 2C Handling data and problem solving
CPM Framework 3Nc3, 3Dh1, 3Dh2, 3Ps4; CPM Teacher's Resource 20.2, 20.3

Multiply first

Remember

When you multiply by 10, each one becomes a ten and each 10 become a hundred.
Write a zero in the ones space to ensure that each digit is in the correct place for its value.

H	T	U
	2	5
2	5	0

You will need:
resource 4, page 76

Vocabulary
add, digit, multiply, two-digit number, <, >

Shuffle a set of digit cards. Turn over the top two cards and write the numbers in the first set of boxes to create a two-digit number.

Multiply that number by 10 and record the answer in the space shown.
Now turn over 2 more digit cards to create another two-digit number to add to the multiplied number. Record the total. The first one has been done for you.

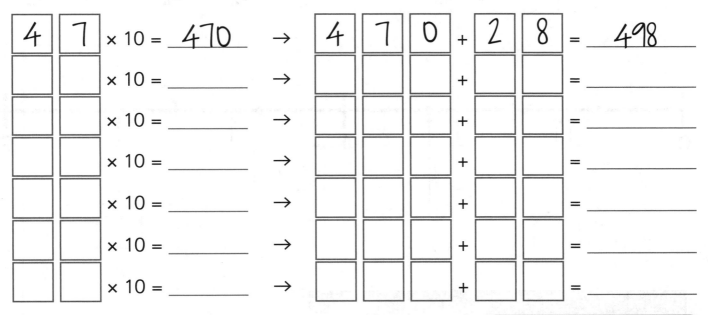

Shuffle the cards and repeat the activity.

Mark each total on the number line.

Hint: Use a number line to help order the totals.

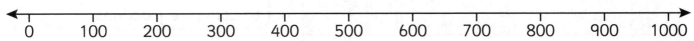

Write 6 different number statements comparing the numbers you have marked on the number line, for example, 367 < 832 and 671 > 235

Unit 3A Number and problem solving
CPM Framework 3Nn7, 3Nn11, 3Nn12, 3Pt1, 3Pt3, 3Ps3; CPM Teacher's Resource 21.1, 21.2

51

Fraction number lines

Remember

A mixed number is a number made from a whole number and a fraction, for example $3\frac{1}{2}$.

Vocabulary

mixed number, whole, fraction, half, third, quarter, eighth

Complete each number line.

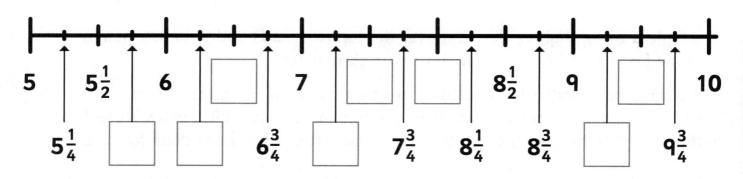

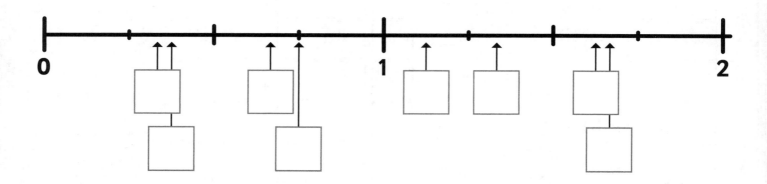

1									
$\frac{1}{2}$					$\frac{1}{2}$				
$\frac{1}{3}$			$\frac{1}{3}$			$\frac{1}{3}$			
$\frac{1}{4}$		$\frac{1}{4}$		$\frac{1}{4}$			$\frac{1}{4}$		
$\frac{1}{8}$	$\frac{1}{8}$	$\frac{1}{8}$	$\frac{1}{8}$	$\frac{1}{8}$	$\frac{1}{8}$	$\frac{1}{8}$	$\frac{1}{8}$		
$\frac{1}{10}$	$\frac{1}{10}$	$\frac{1}{10}$	$\frac{1}{10}$	$\frac{1}{10}$	$\frac{1}{10}$	$\frac{1}{10}$	$\frac{1}{10}$	$\frac{1}{10}$	$\frac{1}{10}$

Hint: Use a fraction wall to compare fractions.

Unit 3A Number and problem solving
CPM Framework 3Nn15, 3Nn16, 3Nn17, 3Nn18, 3Nn19, 3Nn20, 3Ps3; CPM Teacher's Resource 22.1, 22.3, 22.4

Tangram fractions

Remember

A mixed number is a number made from a whole number and a fraction, for example $3\frac{1}{2}$.

You will need:
resource 5, page 77, scissors

Vocabulary
whole, fraction, half, quarter, eighth, sixteenth

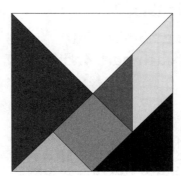

What fraction of the whole is each piece of the tangram?

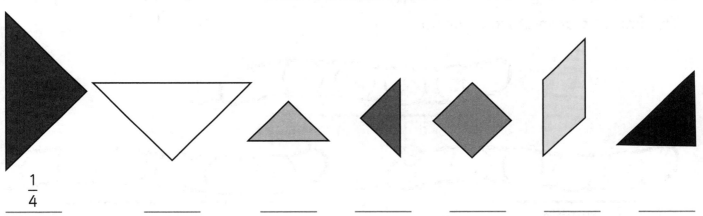

$\frac{1}{4}$

_____

The tangram is 1 whole square.
The total of all the fractions must also be 1. Complete the number sentence.

$\frac{1}{4}$ + _____ + _____ + _____ + _____ + _____ + _____ = **1**

Hint: Cut out the tangram pieces. Place small triangles on top of the square and parallelogram to find the fraction value of each piece.

Unit 3A Number and problem solving
CPM Framework 3Nn15, 3Nn16, 3Nn20, 3Ps3; CPM Teacher's Resource 22.1, 22.2, 22.3, 22.4

53

Doubling and halving snakes

Remember

To **double** a number, partition the number into hundreds, tens and ones. Double each part and add them together to find the double.

To **halve** a number, partition the number into hundreds, tens and ones. Halve each part and add them together to find half.

Vocabulary
double, half, halve, halving

Hint: Doubling is the same as multiplying by 2. Halving is the same as dividing by 2. Doubling and halving are the inverse of each other.

Follow the instructions to complete each snake. Some are doubling snakes, some are halving snakes.

The first has been started for you.

15 30 60

double

50

double

40

halve

800

halve

10

double

45

double

25

double

280

halve

100

halve

Now read the numbers on each snake from the tail to the head and then from the head to the tail. What do you notice?

Unit 3A Number and problem solving
CPM Framework 3Nc6, 3Nc7, 3Nc8, 3Nn14, 3Pt1, 3Pt12, 3Ps3, 3Ps6; CPM Teacher's Resource 23.1

Complements cross-number puzzle

Remember
To find the **complement** to 100 of a number, subtract the number from 100. The difference is the complement of the number.

You will need: a hundred square

Vocabulary
subtract, complement, difference

The answer to each clue is the complement to 100 for that number.

Hint: Think about where each number is, on a 100 square. The number of squares that will take you to 100 is the **complement to 100** of that number.

Across

1 73		**7** 26	
2 25		**8** 81	
3 59		**9** 49	
4 68		**10** 43	
5 53			

Down

1 79		**5** 56	
2 28		**6** 11	
3 52		**7** 29	
4 63		**8** 83	

Remainders collector

Remember
When one number is divided by another number, it may not divide exactly. The amount left over is called the remainder. For example, 23 ÷ 3 = 7 r2. There are 7 groups of 3 in 23, with 2 left over.

You will need:
a 1–6 dice, counters in two different colours

Vocabulary
divide, division, remainder

This is a game for two players.

Take turns to roll the dice and move around the board in any direction.
Work out the division calculation to find the remainder. Either place a counter on the remainder in your collector card or cross it out, unless you have already collected that number.

Once your collector card is complete, return to the start. The winner is the first player to return to the start with a completed collector card.

Player 1 collector card		
1	2	3
4	5	6
7	8	9

Player 2 collector card		
1	2	3
4	5	6
7	8	9

Hint: Use multiplication or division tables to help you work out the division calculations quickly.

25 ÷ 20	58 ÷
17 ÷ 5	
73 ÷ 10	
95 ÷ 10	
28 ÷ 10	
22 ÷ 4	39 ÷
43 ÷ 4	
50 ÷ 9	
35 ÷ 9	
22 ÷ 10	
20 ÷ 3	27 ÷

Unit 3A Number and problem solving
CPM Framework 3Nc21, 3Nc26, 3Pt1, 3Pt3, 3Ps3; CPM Teacher's Resource 25.3

3 ÷ 9	33 ÷ 10	29 ÷ 3	27 ÷ 2	88 ÷ 10	60 ÷ 9	74 ÷ 10	42 ÷ 5	29 ÷ 2
			54 ÷ 5					79 ÷ 10
			87 ÷ 9					70 ÷ 9
			25 ÷ 9					44 ÷ 10
			71 ÷ 9					34 ÷ 4
÷ 10	36 ÷ 10	99 ÷ 10	**Start and Finish**	89 ÷ 10	56 ÷ 10	25 ÷ 10	40 ÷ 6	23 ÷ 2
			44 ÷ 9					69 ÷ 10
			34 ÷ 9					37 ÷ 10
			66 ÷ 10					29 ÷ 6
			52 ÷ 6					23 ÷ 5
1 ÷ 9	57 ÷ 10	49 ÷ 10	27 ÷ 2	48 ÷ 5	35 ÷ 6	77 ÷ 10	59 ÷ 10	21 ÷ 2

Name that shape

Remember

2D shapes are named by the number of sides and corners (vertices). In a **regular** shape, all the sides are equal in length and all the angles are the same size. In an **irregular** shape, the sides can be different lengths and the angles can be different sizes.

A **right angle** is a square corner, like the angles in a square.

A **symmetrical** shape has at least one **line of symmetry**. Each side of the line of symmetry is an identical reflection of the other side. Shapes can have more than 1 line of symmetry.

You will need: a 1–6 dice, a counter for each player, 2D shapes, a setsquare, a ruler, paper and pencil

Vocabulary

2D shape, regular, irregular, draw, curved, straight, circle, triangle, square, rectangle, quadrilateral, pentagon, hexagon, octagon, right angle, symmetry, line of symmetry, reflection

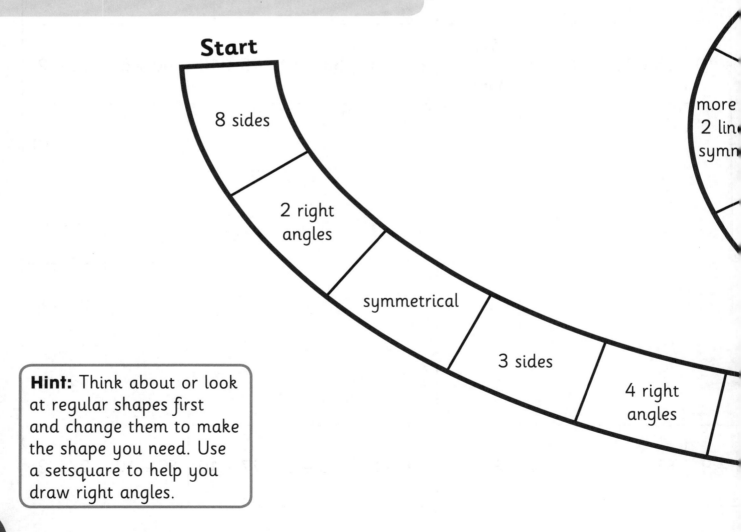

Start

8 sides

2 right angles

symmetrical

3 sides

4 right angles

more 2 lin symm

Hint: Think about or look at regular shapes first and change them to make the shape you need. Use a setsquare to help you draw right angles.

Unit 3B Geometry and problem solving
CPM Framework 3Gs1, 3Gs2, 3Gs5, 3Gs6, 3Gs8; CPM Teacher's Resource 26.1

Players take turns to roll the dice and move their counter along the track.
Draw and name a shape that matches the description on the square you land on.
It could be a regular or irregular shape. If your partner agrees that your shape
matches the description, stay where you are. If the shape is incorrect, move back
3 spaces.
The winner is the first player to reach the finish.

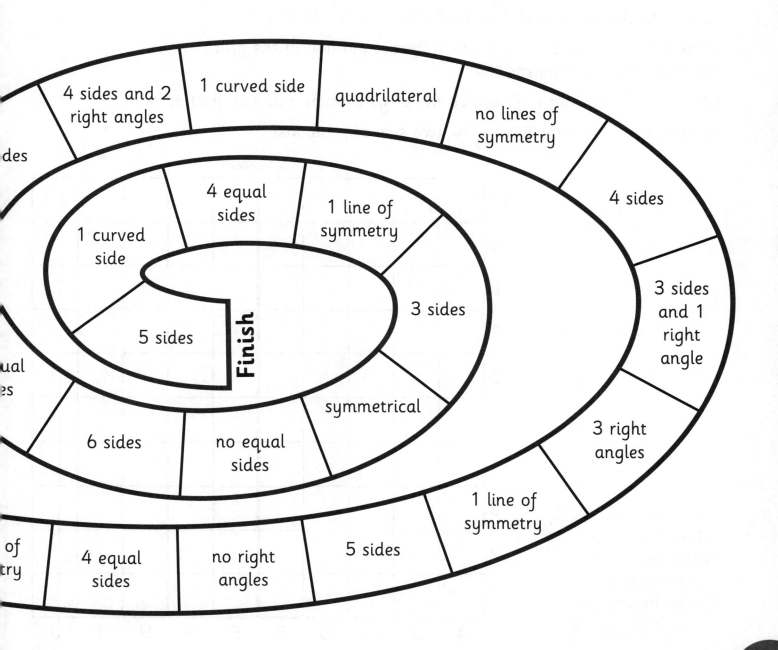

Reflected letters

Remember
Numbers and letters can be used to describe the position of a square on a grid of squares. The letter describes the number of squares along the bottom of the grid and the number describes the number of squares up the grid.

You will need: a ruler

Vocabulary
symmetry, line of symmetry, reflection, coordinates

Draw a capital letter made from squares in the first half of the grid.
You could choose E, F, H, I, L, M, N, O, T, V, W, X, Y or Z.

Draw the reflection of your letter in the second half of the grid.
The thick line is the mirror line.

What are the positions of each corner of your letter and its reflection?

Are there any patterns linking the two sets of positions?

Hint: Draw the letter on squares on a piece of scrap paper before you draw it in the grid.

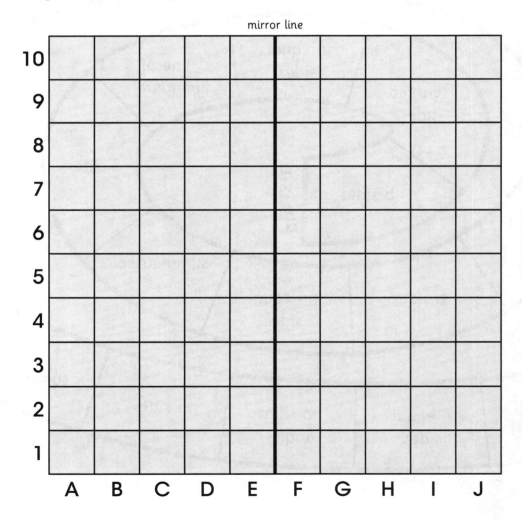

Unit 3B Geometry and problem solving
CPM Framework 3Gs1, 3Gs5, 3Gs7, 3Gp2, 3Ps6; CPM Teacher's Resource 27.1, 28.2

Travelling times

Remember

There are 60 minutes in an hour.
Times between midnight and midday are called am,
times between midday and midnight are called pm.

You will need: a digital clock (if available), a number line

Vocabulary
time, minute, hour, am, pm

1 You arrived at 5:39 pm and
   waited until quarter past 6 in the evening.

   How long did you wait?

2 The train left at 6:23 am and arrived at 8 minutes to 7 am.

   How long did the journey take?

3 The coach left at 9:24 am and arrived at 3:48 pm.

   How long did the journey take?

4 The train left at 3:15 pm and arrived at 5:03 pm.

   How long did the journey take?

5 You arrived early to catch the 9:52 am train. If you arrived at 9:18 am,

   how long did you have to wait?

6 Coaches leave every hour at 20 past the hour. You missed the 4:20 pm coach by

   11 minutes. How long do you have to wait for the next one?

7 The 10:35 am train arrived at 11:21 am.

   How many minutes late was it?

8 The flight left at 1:58 pm and arrived at 5:16 pm.

   How long was the flight?

Order the times from shortest to longest.

Hint: Work out how many minutes to the next hour, then how many more minutes or hours.

Unit 3C Measure and problem solving
CPM Framework 3Mt1, 3Mt2, 3Mt3, 3Pt1, 3Pt2; CPM Teacher's Resource 29.1, 29.2

Hole in my pocket

Remember
100c = $1

 = $1

You will need:
a coloured counter for each player, real or plastic currency (optional)

Vocabulary
coin, note, cent, dollar, amount, deduct, subtract

This is a game for two players.

Start with $20 each. Take turns to spin the spinner and move your counter that many spaces along the track. Each amount that you land on must be deducted (subtracted) from your original $20. The player with more money left when both players have reached **Finish** is the winner.

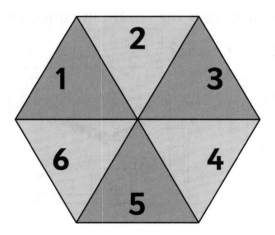

Hint: Use real or plastic currency to help you work out how much money you have left. Deduct the matching amount each turn.

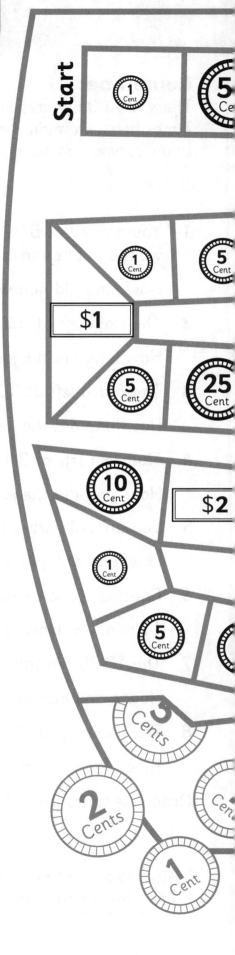

Unit 3C Measure and problem solving
CPM Framework 3Mm1, 3Mm2, 3Pt1, 3Ps2; CPM Teacher's Resource 30.1

Collect the milk

You will need:
a 1–6 dice, a coloured counter for each player

Remember
1000 millilitres = 1 litre

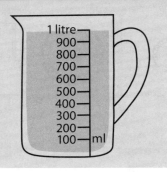

1 litre
900
800
700
600
500
400
300
200
100 — ml

Vocabulary
amount, millilitre, litre

How many litres of goat's milk can you collect?
The winner is the player who has collected more.

Take turns to roll the dice and move your counter
along the track. Collect the amount you land on.
Add the amounts together to find out how much
you have collected.

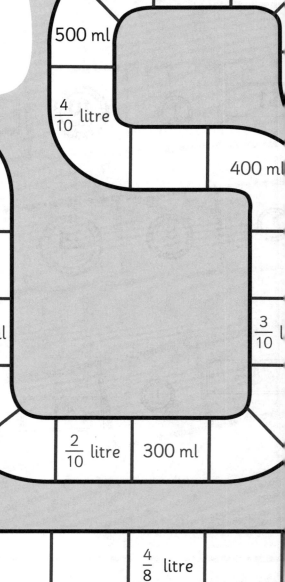

$\frac{5}{10}$ litre

500 ml

$\frac{4}{10}$ litre

400 ml

Entrance and Exit

100 ml

$\frac{1}{10}$ litre

800 ml

$\frac{6}{8}$ litre

200 ml

$\frac{3}{10}$ l

$\frac{2}{10}$ litre

300 ml

700 ml

$\frac{2}{8}$ litre

600 ml

$\frac{4}{8}$ litre

Unit 3C Measure and problem solving
CPM Framework 3Nn15, 3Nn20, 3Ml2, 3Ml5, 3Pt1, 3Pt2, 3Ps2; CPM Teacher's Resource 31.1

Hint: Convert fractions of a litre to millilitres to make the amounts easier to add. Add each new amount to what you have already collected rather than waiting until the end of the game.

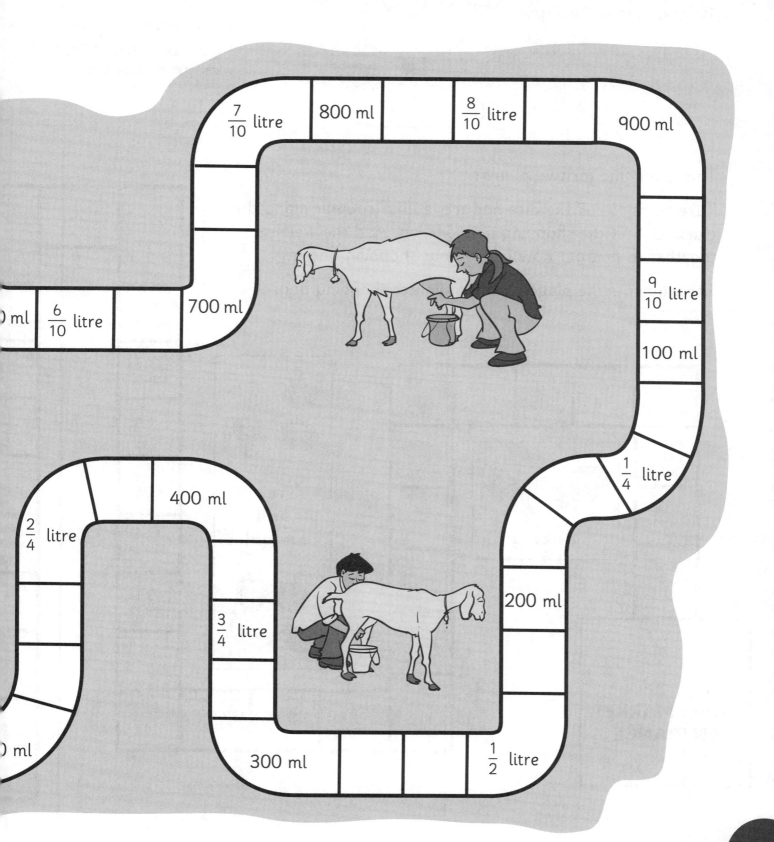

Unit 3C Measure and problem solving
CPM Framework 3Nn15, 3Nn17, 3Nn20, 3MI2, 3MI5, 3Pt1, 3Pt2, 3Ps2; CPM Teacher's Resource 31.1

65

Shopping bags

Remember

1000 grams = 1 kilogram

You will need:
a 1–6 dice, a coloured counter for each player

Vocabulary

heavy, light, weigh, weight, mass, gram, kilogram

This is a game for two players.

Take turns to roll the dice and move your counter along the track. Collect the shopping you land on. Add the weights together to find out how heavy your shopping bag is.

The winner is the player with the lighter shopping bag.

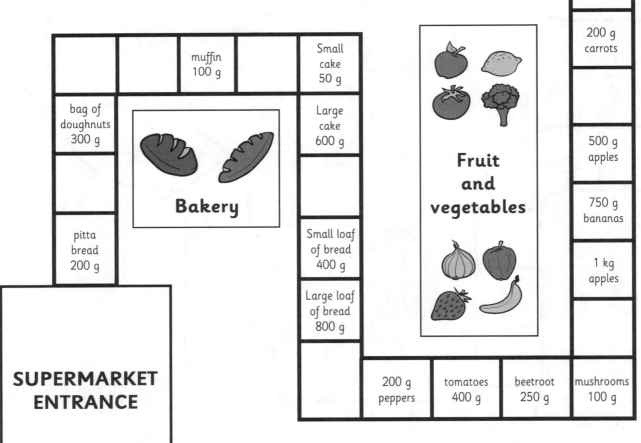

Unit 3C Measure and problem solving
CPM Framework 3MI1, 3MI2, 3MI5, 3Pt1, 3Pt2, 3Ps2; CPM Teacher's Resource 32.1, 32.2

Hint: Add each new weight to what you have already collected, rather than waiting until the end of the game.

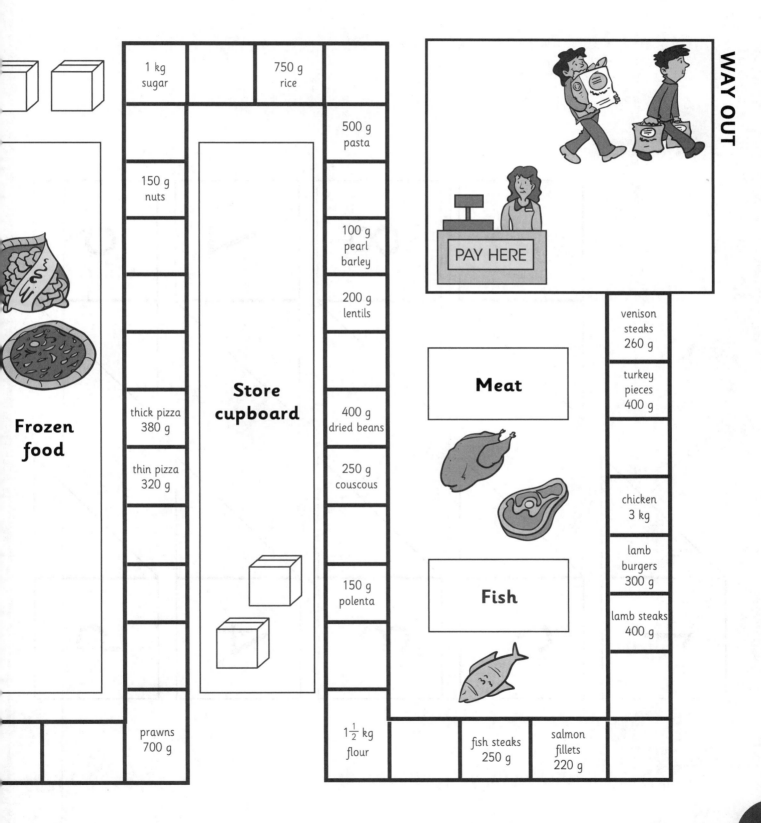

WAY OUT

1 kg sugar

750 g rice

500 g pasta

150 g nuts

100 g pearl barley

200 g lentils

PAY HERE

venison steaks 260 g

turkey pieces 400 g

Meat

Frozen food

thick pizza 380 g

Store cupboard

400 g dried beans

thin pizza 320 g

250 g couscous

chicken 3 kg

lamb burgers 300 g

150 g polenta

Fish

lamb steaks 400 g

prawns 700 g

1½ kg flour

fish steaks 250 g

salmon fillets 220 g

Unit 3C Measure and problem solving
CPM Framework 3MI1, 3MI2, 3MI5, 3Pt1, 3Pt2, 3Ps2; CPM Teacher's Resource 32.1, 32.2

67

Resource 1
Place-value cards

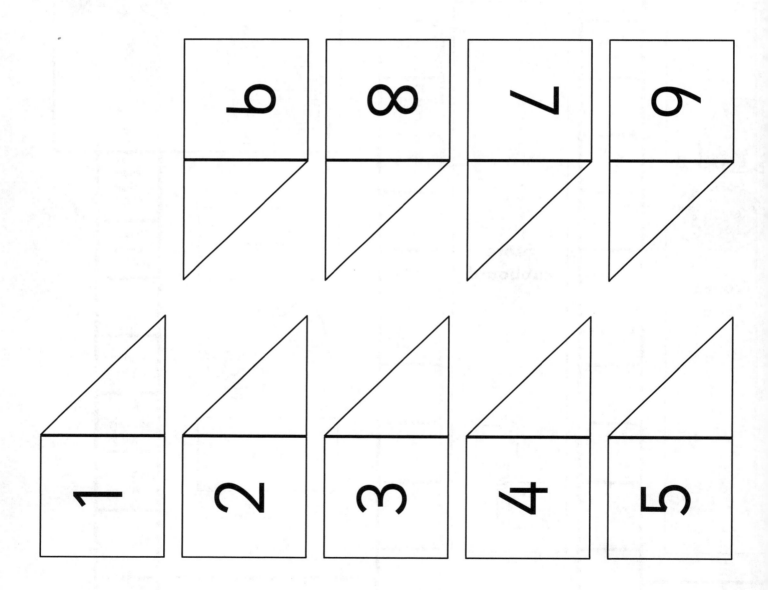

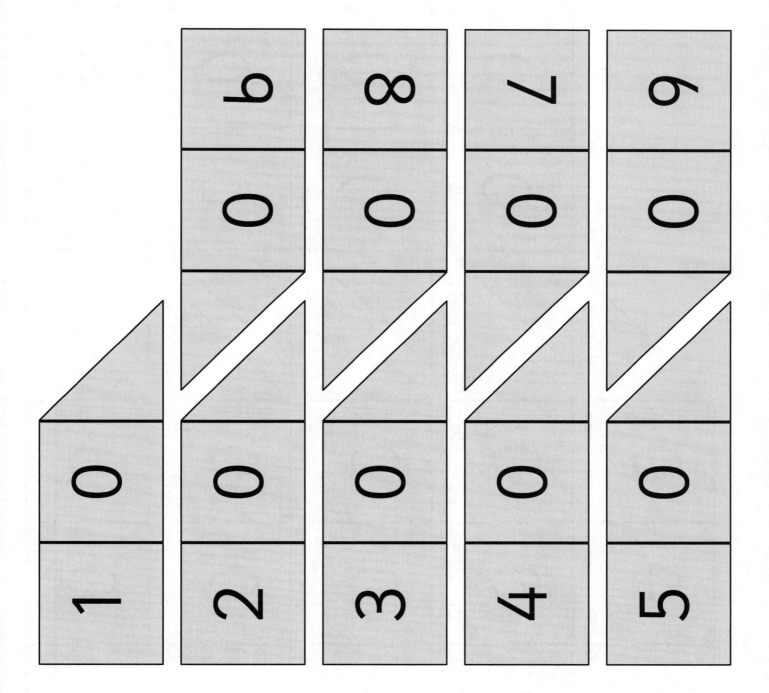

9 0 0

8 0 0

7 0 0

6 0 0

1 0 0

2 0 0

3 0 0

4 0 0

5 0 0

Photocopiable resources

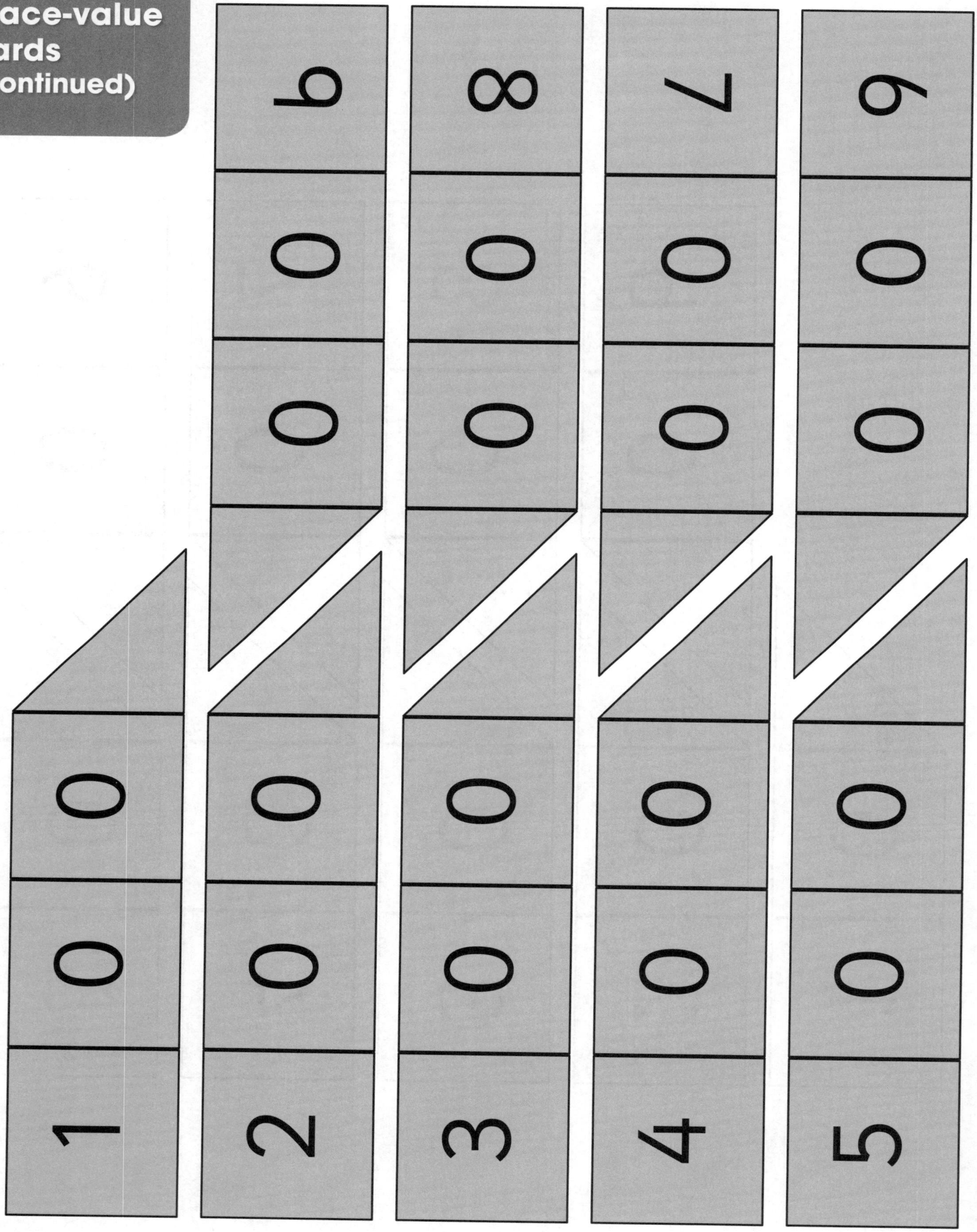

Original material © Cambridge University Press 2016

Resource 2
Squares and triangles

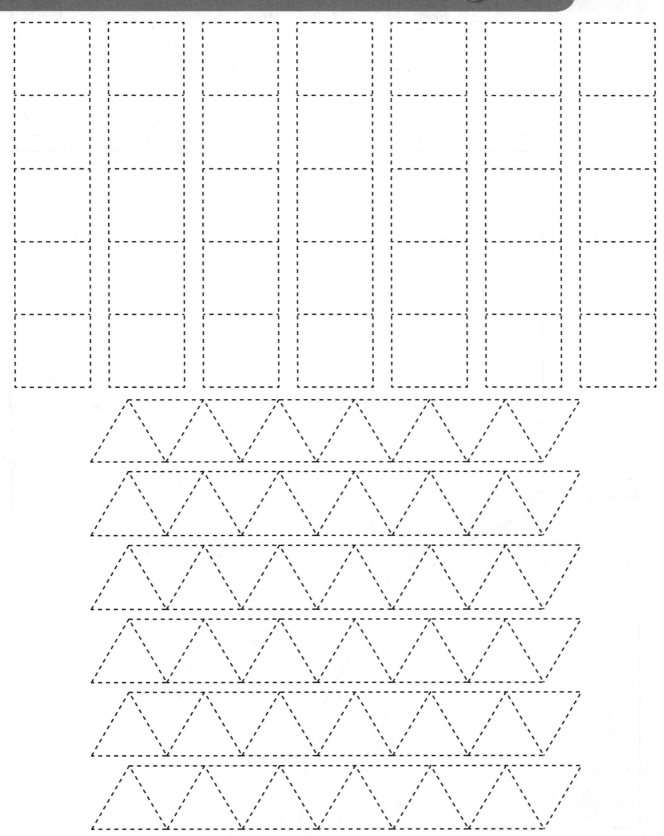

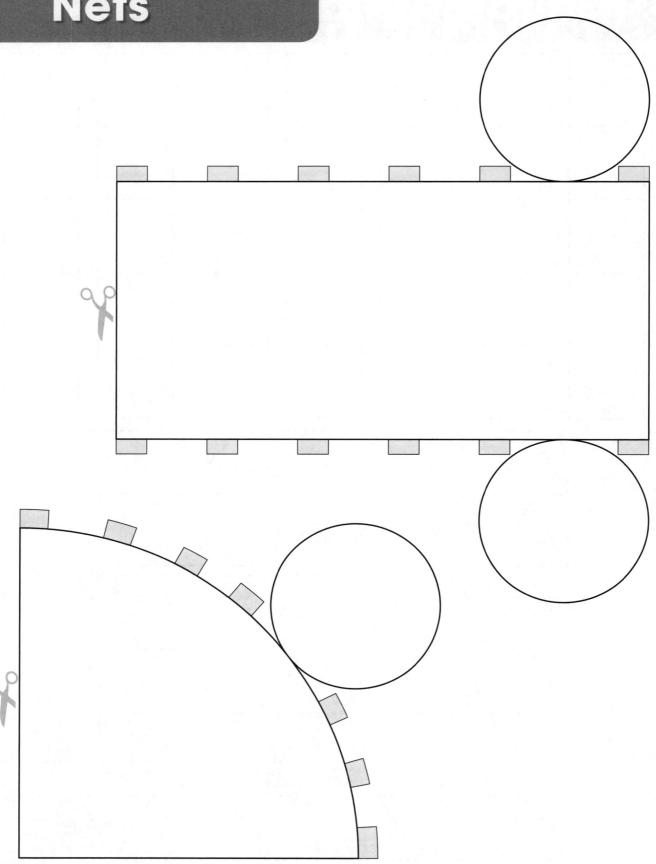

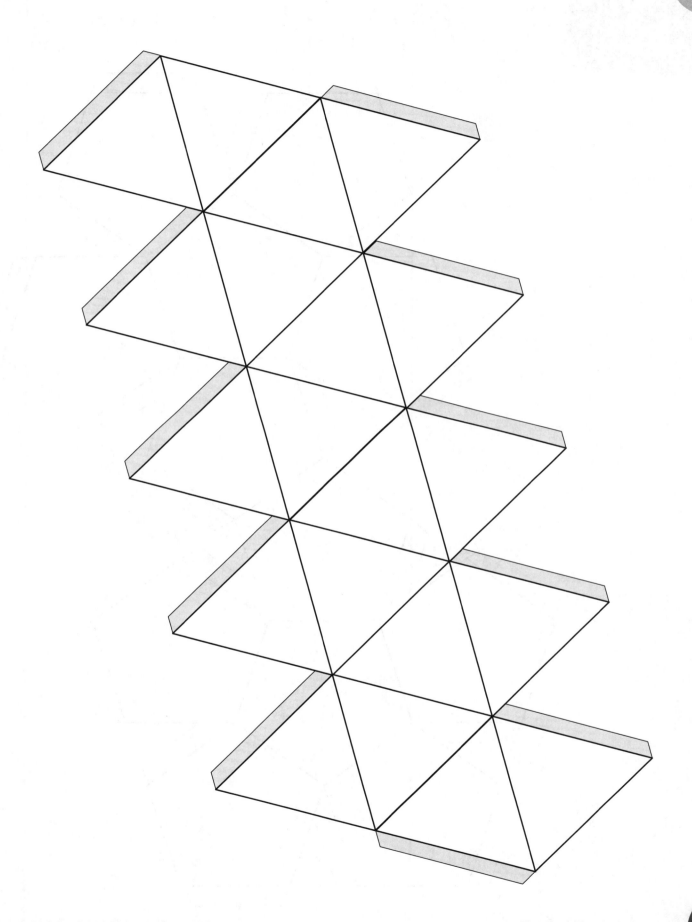

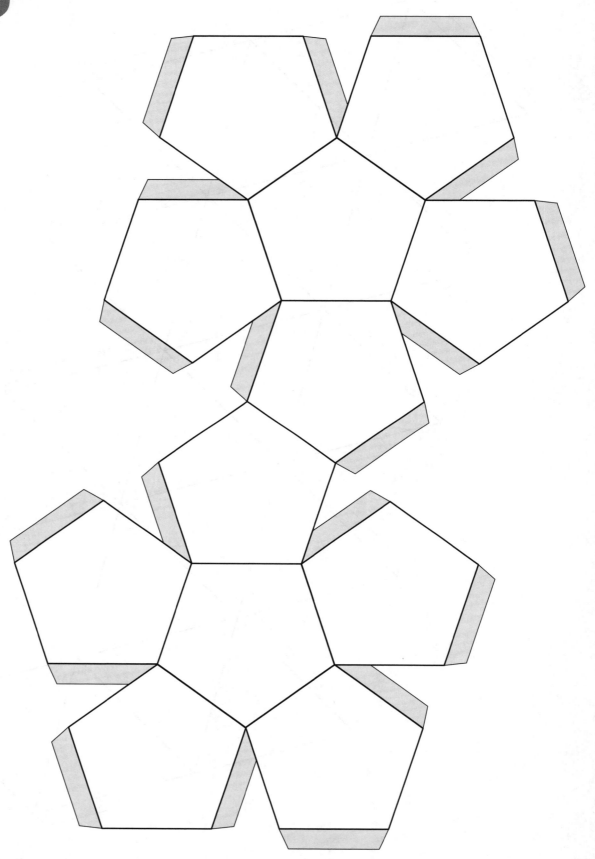

Photocopiable resources

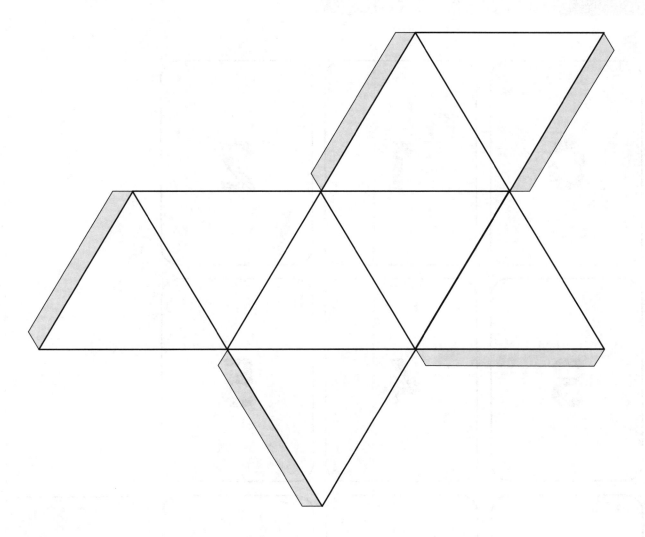

Resource 4
Digit cards

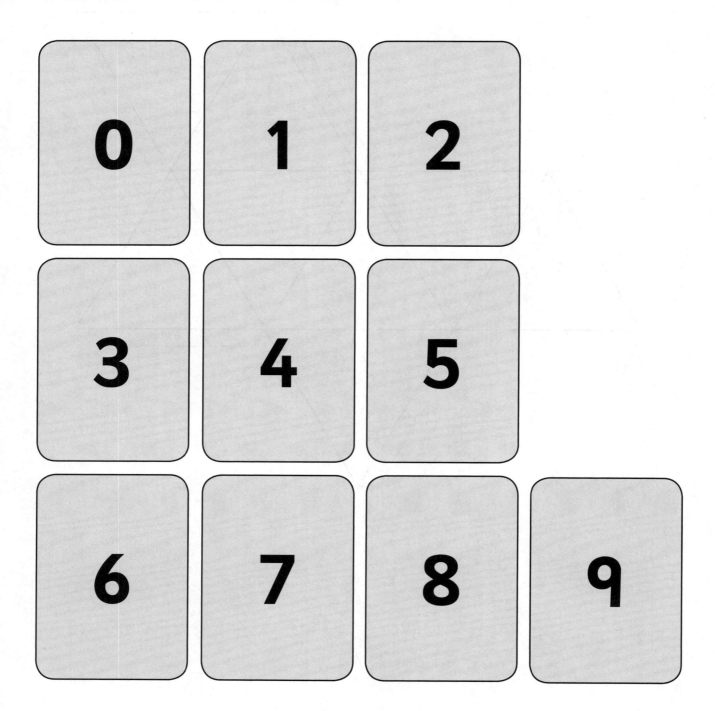

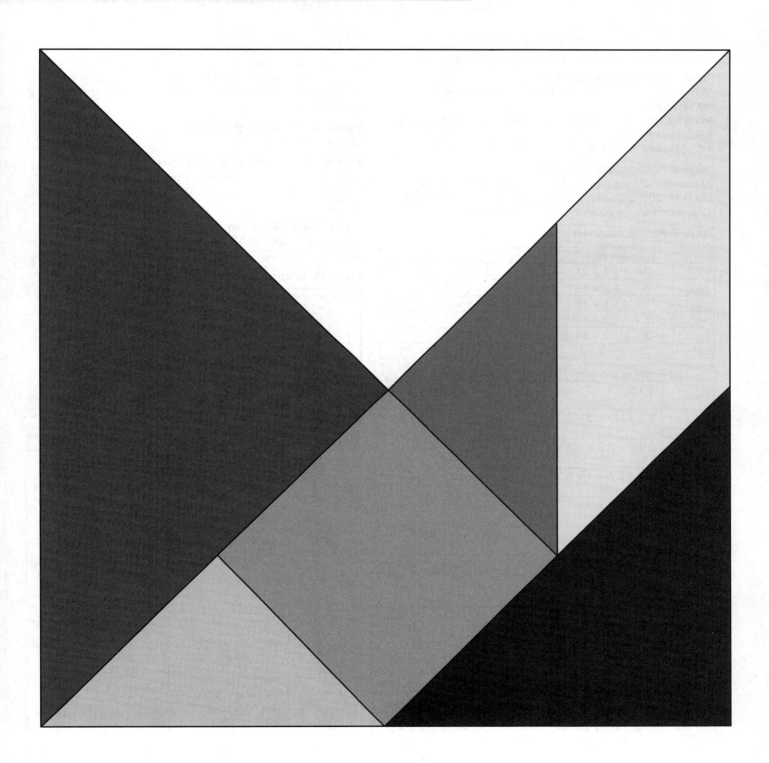

Answers

Page 4 Three-digit numbers
The 20 and 7 from set 1 have been swapped with the 30 and 9 from set 2.
10 less: 90 would be left over.
10 more: Although 10 would be left over, another hundreds place-value card or possibly a 1000 would be needed.

Page 6 Twelve abacus beads
All numbers with digits that add to make 12 can be made since each one needs a bead.
Any numbers in which the digits add to more than 12, for example 654, cannot be made.
840, 741, 642, 543, 444, 345, 246, 147, 48

Page 7 Palindromic numbers
20 palindromic numbers: 101, 111, 121, 131, 141, 151, 161, 171, 181, 191, 202, 212, 222, 232, 242, 252, 262, 272, 282, 292.
4 non-palindromic numbers: 91, 192, 201 and 302.

Page 8 Phone numbers

3-letter words		4-letter words	
sum	7 + 8 + 6 = 21	even	3 + 8 + 3 + 6 = 20
map	6 + 2 + 7 = 15	hour	4 + 6 + 8 + 7 = 25
nil	6 + 4 + 5 = 15	zero	9 + 3 + 7 + 6 = 25
odd	6 + 3 + 3 = 12	dice	3 + 4 + 2 + 3 = 12
day	3 + 2 + 9 = 14	cube	2 + 8 + 2 + 3 = 15
add	2 + 3 + 3 = 8	side	7 + 4 + 3 + 3 = 17

5-letter words		6-letter words	
equal	3 + 7 + 8 + 2 + 5 = 25	abacus	2 + 2 + 2 + 2 + 8 + 7 = 23
array	2 + 7 + 7 + 2 + 9 = 27	answer	2 + 6 + 7 + 9 + 3 + 7 = 34
count	2 + 6 + 8 + 6 + 8 = 30	change	3 + 4 + 2 + 6 + 4 + 3 = 22
digit	3 + 4 + 4 + 4 + 8 = 23	corner	2 + 6 + 7 + 6 + 3 + 7 = 31
money	6 + 6 + 6 + 3 + 9 = 30	double	3 + 6 + 8 + 2 + 5 + 3 = 27
metre	6 + 3 + 8 + 7 + 3 = 27	puzzle	7 + 8 + 9 + 9 + 5 + 3 = 41

7-letter words		More than 7 letters	
balance	2 + 2 + 5 + 2 + 6 + 2 + 3 = 22	addition	2 + 3 + 3 + 4 + 8 + 4 + 6 + 6 = 36
between	2 + 3 + 8 + 9 + 3 + 3 + 6 = 34	subtraction	7 + 8 + 2 + 8 + 7 + 2 + 2 + 8 + 4 + 6 + 6 = 60
biggest	2 + 4 + 4 + 4 + 3 + 7 + 8 = 32	multiplication	6 + 8 + 5 + 8 + 4 + 7 + 5 + 4 + 2 + 2 + 8 + 4 + 6 + 6 = 75
compare	2 + 6 + 6 + 7 + 2 + 7 + 3 = 33	division	3 + 4 + 8 + 4 + 7 + 4 + 6 + 6 = 42
largest	5 + 2 + 7 + 4 + 3 + 7 + 8 = 36	rectangle	7 + 3 + 2 + 8 + 2 + 6 + 4 + 5 + 3 = 40
explain	3 + 9 + 7 + 5 + 2 + 4 + 6 = 36	quadrilateral	7 + 8 + 2 + 3 + 7 + 4 + 5 + 2 + 8 + 3 + 7 + 2 + 5 = 63

Is **odd** worth less than **even**? Yes, odd = 12, even = 20.
Is **nil** worth more than **zero**? No, nil = 15, zero = 25.

Is **dice** worth less than **cube**? Yes, dice = 12, cube = 15.
Is **biggest** worth more than **largest**? No, largest = 36, biggest = 32.

Page 10 Spiders in the bath
Doubling: 6, 12, 24, 48, 96, 192, 384, 768.
Halving: 384, 192, 96, 48, 24, 12, 6, 3. 3 spiders left on day 8.
Each halving undoes the doubling, so it takes the same amount of time to get back to 3 spiders as it did to get to 768 because halving is the inverse of doubling.

Page 12 Calculating spiders
Children's own answers.

Pages 14–15 Hundreds and thousands
Game. Correct number sentences are the number pairs that are multiples of 100 with a total of 1000 and multiple of 5 with a total of 100.

Pages 16–17 River crossing
Missing: 7, 11, 13, 14, 17, 18, 19, 21, 23. Only the first 5 multiples of the 1, 2, 3, 4 and 5 multiplication tables are on the river crossing.

Page 19 Multiples of 3 and 4

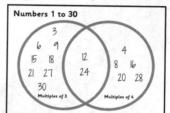

The numbers in the overlap are multiples of 3 AND multiples of 4.

Page 20 Same and different
Possible answers include:

Shapes	What is the same?	What is different?
	Both have 6 faces and 12 edges.	Cube has square faces. Cuboid has rectangular faces, but some faces could be squares.
	Both have at least 1 circular face. Both have a curved surface (or face).	Cylinder has 2 edges and no vertices. Cone has 1 edge and 1 vertex (or apex).
	Both have a curved surface (or face) and no vertices.	A sphere has no edges. A cylinder has 2 edges.
	Both are pyramids and have triangular faces.	A square based pyramid has one square face. All the triangular based pyramid faces are the same.
	Both have 5 faces. Both have some triangular faces.	Triangular prism has 9 edges. Square based pyramid has 8 edges.
	Both have some rectangular or square faces.	A hexagonal based prism has twice as many edges as a triangular based prism.
Children's choice	Children's own answers.	Children's own answers.

Page 25 Planet Xylo
Children's own solutions, each with a total of 24 faces.

Page 26 Nets
Cylinder, cone, octahedron, icosahedron and dodecahedron.

Page 27 Symmetrical flags
Lines of symmetry

0	2	0
2	1	1
2	0	2
1	2	2

Page 28 Pocket money

Week	Doubling	Weekly total	$5 a week	Weekly total
1	1c	1c	$5	$5
2	2c	3c	$5	$10
3	4c	7c	$5	$15
4	8c	15c	$5	$20
5	16c	31c	$5	$25
6	32c	63c	$5	$30
7	64c	$1.27	$5	$35
8	$1.28	$2.55	$5	$40
9	$2.56	$5.11	$5	$45
10	$5.12	$10.23	$5	$50
11	$10.24	$20.47	$5	$55
12	$20.48	$40.95	$5	$60
13	$40.96	$81.91	$5	$65
14	$81.92	$163.83	$5	$70
15	$163.84	$327.67	$5	$75
16	$327.68	$655.35	$5	$80
17	$655.36	$1310.71	$5	$85
18	$1310.72	$2621.43	$5	$90
19	$2621.44	$5242.87	$5	$95
20	$52.42.88	$10485.75	$5	$100

Page 31 Cross-number puzzle

¹3	6	8		²7	3	1
³9	7		⁴6	2	1	
4		⁵4	0	9		⁶8
	⁷6	1	2		⁸4	2
⁹6	3	1		¹⁰5	5	9
¹¹3	1			¹²2	9	

Page 35 Single, double, treble, quadruple
22 and 26 will not be made.

Page 36 Odd one out

1	39 + 29	41 + 27	⟨84 – 7⟩	80 – 12
2	132 – 60	⟨28 + 45⟩	89 – 17	36 + 36
3	⟨73 + 74⟩	166 – 9	148 + 9	95 + 62
4	242 + 19	207 + 54	⟨269 + 8⟩	254 + 7
5	⟨79 + 56⟩	92 – 69	81 – 58	65 – 42
6	27 + 58	64 + 21	⟨49 + 46⟩	99 – 14
7	298 + 7	313 – 8	297 + 8	⟨302 + 4⟩
8	⟨99 – 6⟩	41 + 53	100 – 6	103 – 9
9	505 – 9	⟨423 + 83⟩	451 + 45	502 – 6
10	32 + 27	83 – 24	91 – 32	⟨29 + 29⟩

Pages 38–39 Multiplication pyramids

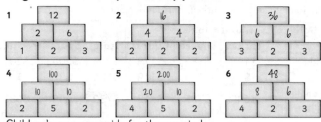

Children's own pyramids for the remainder.

Page 42 A question of time
The correct time is 7:47; 16 nights; 960 minutes.

Page 43 Days and dates
5 days from today? Tuesday
11 days from today? Monday
21 days from today? Thursday
40 days from today? Tuesday
70 days from today? Thursday
1 day
14th May

Page 44 Estimate and measure
Length of a **car**
1 metre ⟨**4 metres**⟩ 8 metres
Capacity of a **mug**
3 litres   30 millilitres ⟨**300 millilitres**⟩
Height of an **elephant**
30 centemetres ⟨**3 metres**⟩ 3 kilometres
Weight of an **egg**
6 grams ⟨**60 grams**⟩ 600 grams
Length of a **mobile phone**
5 centimetres ⟨**12 centimetres**⟩ 20 centimetres
Weight of an **apple**
⟨**100 grams**⟩ 10 grams   1 kilogram
Capacity of a **teapot**
1 millilitre ⟨**1 litre**⟩ 10 litres
Weight of a **new born baby**
40 kilograms   400 grams ⟨**4 kilograms**⟩
Capacity of a **bath**
400 millilitres   4 litres ⟨**200 litres**⟩

Page 46 Money problems

	Month 1	Month 2	Month 3
$24	$24 – $12 = $12	$12 + $24 = $36 $36 – $18 = $18	$18 + $24 = $42 $42 – $21 = $21
$30	$30 – $15 = $15	$15 + $30 = $45 $45 – $22.50 = $22.50	$22.50 + $30 = $52.50 $52.50 – $26.25 = $26.25
$36	$36 – $18 = $18	$18 + $36 = $54 $54 – $27 = $27	$27 + $36 = $63 $63 – $31.50 = $31.50
$40	$40 – $20 = $20	$20 + $40 = $60 $60 – $30 = $30	$30 + $40 = $70 $70 – $35 = $35

3 25c stamps = 75c and 4 19c stamps = 76c.
Total spend $1.51, 49c change.

Page 47 Holiday time

The family can go to Turkey, Portugal or Spain.

Flight costs, round trip						
Place	Turkey	Greece	Cyprus	Italy	Spain	Portugal
Adult	$199	$189	$179	$209	$204	$201
Child	$99	$109	$119	$104	$97	$95
Family return cost	**$695**	$705	$715	$730	**$699**	**$687**

Page 48–49 At the funfair

Ride	Tally	Frequency
Carousel	ЖHТ ЖHТ ЖHТ III	18
Bumper cars	ЖHТ ЖHТ ЖHТ	15
Ferris wheel	ЖHТ ЖHТ ЖHТ III	23
Helter skelter	ЖHТ ЖHТ IIII	14
Roller coaster	ЖHТ ЖHТ ЖHТ ЖHТ ЖHТ III	28
Teacups	ЖHТ ЖHТ II	12
Waltzers	ЖHТ ЖHТ ЖHТ ЖHТ I	21
Drop tower	ЖHТ ЖHТ ЖHТ ЖHТ ЖHТ ЖHТ I	31
Pirate ship	ЖHТ ЖHТ ЖHТ ЖHТ ЖHТ II	27

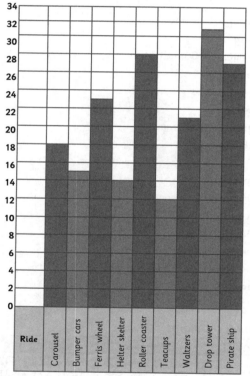

The owner should close the Teacups, the Helter skelter and the Bumper cars because they had the fewest customers.

Page 52 Fraction number lines

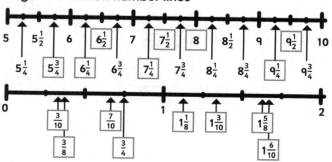

Page 53 Tangram fractions

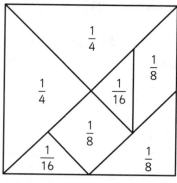

$$\frac{1}{4} + \frac{1}{4} + \frac{1}{16} + \frac{1}{16} + \frac{1}{8} + \frac{1}{8} + \frac{1}{8} = 1$$

Page 54 Doubling and halving snakes

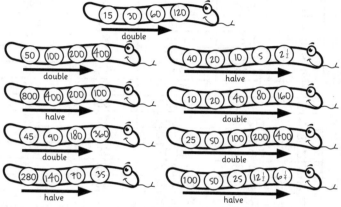

Doubling and halving are opposites, the inverse of each other. So doubling starting at 50 gives you the same numbers as halving starting at 800.

(So the doubling snake 50, 100, 200, 400 reads 400, 200, 100, 50 (halving) in the other direction and the halving snake 800, 400, 200, 100 reads 100, 200, 400, 800 (doubling) in the other direction.)

Page 55 Complements cross-number puzzle

	2	7		7	5
4	1		3	2	
8		4	7		8
	7	4		1	9
5	1		5	7	

Page 61 Travelling times

1 36 minutes
2 29 minutes
3 6 hours 24 minutes
4 1 hour 48 minutes
5 34 minutes
6 49 minutes
7 46 minutes
8 3 hours 18 minutes

29 minutes, 34 minutes, 36 minutes, 46 minutes, 49 minutes, 1 hour 48 minutes, 3 hours 18 minutes, 6 hours 24 minutes.

CAMBRIDGE PRIMARY
Mathematics

Challenge 3

Cambridge Primary Mathematics **Challenge** Activity Books are the latest addition to the Cambridge Primary Mathematics course. This is a flexible and engaging course written specifically for the Cambridge Primary Mathematics curriculum framework Stages I to 6. The course offers a discussion-led approach with problem-solving integrated throughout to encourage learners to think and talk about mathematics in place of rote learning and drill practice. The language throughout the course is pitched to EAL / ESL learners with illustrations supporting visual understanding and learning.

The Challenge Activity Books are carefully designed to provide extension activities for high-achieving children who need more challenging activities to stretch their skills beyond the standard required for success in the Cambridge Primary Mathematics curriculum framework.

Challenge Activity Book 3 consists of:

- A full range of activities which support the breadth of the Cambridge Primary Mathematics curriculum framework at Grade 3.
- Carefully levelled activities which help stretch and deepen a child's mathematical understanding and performance beyond the standard expected by the framework.
- Helpful guidance and tips to help explain either to the learner or the teacher / parent the key mathematical methods and concepts underpinning each exercise.
- For the first time, this flexible resource offers motivational parents the Cambridge way for Maths work at home.

This resource is endorsed for learner support by Cambridge International Examinations

- ✓ Provides learner support as part of a set of resources for the Cambridge Primary Mathematics curriculum framework from 2011
- ✓ Has passed Cambridge's rigorous quality-assurance process
- ✓ Developed by subject experts
- ✓ For Cambridge schools worldwide

Completely **Cambridge**

Cambridge resources **for** Cambridge qualifications

Cambridge University Press works with Cambridge International Examinations and experienced authors, to produce high-quality endorsed textbooks and software that support Cambridge teachers and encourage Cambridge learners.

Visit **cambridge.org/cambridgeprimary** for information on our full range of Cambridge Primary titles.

CAMBRIDGE
UNIVERSITY PRESS

Achieveme
through
excellence

10251386:
lathematics Chal
aths)

9 781316

MULTI LEVEL MARKETING

THE DEFINITIVE GUIDE TO

America's Top MLM Companies